LIGHTS! CAMERA! FICTION!

A MOVIE LOVER'S GUIDE TO WRITING A NOVEL
BY ALFIE THOMPSON

DATE	SCENE	TAKE

RUNNING PRESS

PHILADELPHIA · LONDON

9   8   7   6   5   4   3   2   1
Digit on the right indicates the number of this printing

Library of Congress Control Number: 2005937394

ISBN-13: 978-0-7624-2401-6
ISBN-10: 0-7624-2401-X

Cover illustration(s) by Dan Page
Typography: Akzidenz Grotesk, Ministry, and Roadkill

This book may be ordered by mail from the publisher.
Please include $2.50 for postage and handling.
But try your bookstore first!

Running Press Book Publishers
125 South Twenty-Second Street
Philadelphia, Pennsylvania 19103-4399

Visit us on the web!
www.runningpress.com

Table of Contents

Foreword

BY MICHAEL HAUGE

This is a terrific book.

Yeah, I know what you're thinking. "Of course he's gonna say that."

I mean, here I have a chance to get my name and the title of my own book on someone else's book cover without doing any of the work. I might even get to plug my Web site, *www.ScreenplayMastery.com* (which, by the way, I would never do, because it might seem tacky). So what am I going to say, that the book sucks?

OK, so don't take my word for it. Right now, stop reading this foreword, and flip to the section entitled "The Introductory Stage" on page 34. I guarantee Alfie Thompson's brilliant analysis of the opening few minutes of *While You Were Sleeping* will give you at least a dozen new ways to establish your characters through action, interaction, description, setting, dialogue, echoing, and identification.

Perhaps you haven't bought this book yet and you're sitting on one of those nice benches at a bookstore, trying to decide if you really need one more book on writing. Well, turn to Chapter Four and read just the opening section about Keanu Reeves's character in *Speed* (a movie I would never even have thought of as an example of character growth). Look at all the cool ways Alfie has found to show a character's need and inner conflict through the concept of inferiority.

Then keep skipping through the pages to glance at the QUICK TIPS contained in boxes throughout the book. I promise you'll realize that no matter how many other writing books you own, you definitely need this one.

Or maybe you've ordered this book from an online bookseller or from the WritersStore.com, but you want to open the pages ever so carefully, so if you don't like it, you can exchange it for that DVD of *The Good, the Bad and the Ugly* you've had your eye on.

Fair enough. Put on some white gloves and read Chapter Ten, where Alfie uses both the novel and film versions of *Jaws* to illustrate all the outstanding principles, guidelines, rules, suggestions, tips, tricks, and tools of the trade she's revealed throughout the book. You'll be so overwhelmed by the sheer volume of great ideas she offers, you'll take off your gloves and start dog-earing the pages.

When I first met Alfie, she was attending one of my screenwriting seminars (all of which are listed at *ScreenplayMastery.com*, by the way). I get a lot of novelists at my lectures and classes who are there because they were told their manuscripts would work better as movies. They've usually been told that by readers who didn't like these authors' novels, but who wanted to sound nice, so they pointed the writers toward Hollywood.

I also have many novelists as consulting clients, because they want to adapt their own published novels into screenplays, or because they want to be both novelists *and* screenwriters. But Alfie was different. She had no real interest in writing a screenplay; she was just there to improve her fiction writing.

So here was a writer who was already selling, and whose work had been published all over the world, who just wanted new ways to strengthen her craft.

I thought this was a great idea. Like movies, great novels are visual—they create vivid, striking images of character, setting, and action. And every writer—novelist, dramatist, or screenwriter—has the same goal: to elicit emotion in the audience. It doesn't matter if that audience is sitting in a theater, plunked in front of a television, or turning the pages of a book; they're all there to feel something wonderful.

As *Lights! Camera! Fiction!* makes crystal clear, the principles and methods movies and screenplays use to captivate their audiences will be just as powerful when applied to your own fiction. So I'm honored that Alfie took something she got from my class, added it to her lifetime of experience and her great understanding of fiction, and is now sharing her wisdom in this amazing book. By looking—really looking—at successful Hollywood movies, she has found some wonderful illustrations of the tools you must have if you want to succeed as a storyteller of any kind.

Even better, she's presented these ideas so clearly, simply, and compellingly that they become easy to understand and apply. By choosing popular, mainstream movies as examples, she makes these concepts accessible to us all, and even makes us want to see these movies again—to see for ourselves what her in-depth analyses of these films have revealed.

Which brings me, I'm afraid, to my one big problem with this book: *It's just as valuable for screenwriters as it is for novelists.*

There isn't a page in this book that doesn't contain an abundance of invaluable tools for making movies more emotional, more meaningful, and more commercial. Which means this book is now competing with mine.

Fortunately for me, the title of this book might make it sound like it's just for novelists. So unless you're a screenwriter who's read all the way to the end of this foreword, I may not have to worry.

For the time being.

But as soon as word gets out that Alfie Thompson has written a book that will greatly improve every writer's chance of selling his or her work, sales of my own book might start to drop. And if they do, I'll know exactly whom to blame. And in retaliation, I've decided I'm going to blatantly mention my Web site, *ScreenplayMastery.com*, after all. So there.

Michael Hauge

www.ScreenplayMastery.com (*ha!*)

Chapter One

Getting Started

Can you watch a movie? Good. Then you are qualified to use the lessons of this book to help you craft the publishable story you want to write.

Every working writer will probably laugh at the thought of learning to write books by watching movies, and I don't blame them. "Yeah, sure! You can also learn to play the piano by watching Liberace; or learn to figure skate by watching the Olympics."

So let's get this out of the way up front. Can you really learn to *write* fiction by *watching* movies?

No. A writer learns to write by writing.

But putting pen to page—or fingers to keyboard—and making words appear isn't tough. Most of us acquire those basic skills in grade school. What's tough for a writer is finding the exact word needed to polish a perfect sentence or to create a specific word picture. Constructing a paragraph that places the strongest emphasis on the most important point takes practice. That kind of writing is an *art*.

Once you master the art of putting together a grammatically correct sentence and finding the right words, the next trick is knowing what thoughts belong in a sentence—and the next and the next—if you want to tell an effective story. That's a whole different thing. That's a *craft*.

And yes, you can learn the craft of storytelling by watching movies. You can learn about the pieces and parts of a good story and how they fit together because movies, like novels and all forms of storytelling, have the same basic elements.

Both use a story *premise,* or question, that leads a character to his adventure. Both establish *characters* and show their *motivation* through a series of scenes. *Plot* puts those scenes in an organized structure that makes the best of the story. The story gives those characters *goals* to achieve, then *conflict* gets in the way of the character achieving them. A skill-ful attention to *details* helps foreshadow things to come, lets the audience *suspend disbelief,* and creates an intensity that keeps the reader turning pages or audiences on the edges of their seats.

Those are the things we can learn about fiction writing from watching movies.

There are seemingly natural-born storytellers. I suspect they absorb by osmosis (from reading) more instinctively than the rest of us, and then are able to better utilize the lessons they learn. Envy them if you want. Emulate them if you can. Read everything you can get your hands on to develop your own ongoing process of osmosis. But don't believe that you can't learn to write entertaining stories if you have to struggle to understand some of the things the natural-born storytellers seem to know instinctively.

That's where this book and the movies we're going to study fit into your process. As any successful writer will tell you, *showing* is much better than just *telling*. So instead of telling you how to put together a great plot, I'm going to show you how someone else did it. Instead of telling you how essential conflict is in molding a story, I'm going to show you scenes with characters in conflict, and give you examples of how the characters react to that conflict.

Movies offer several benefits besides great examples. For most people, strong visual images make learning easier and faster. Movies also come in a compressed form—most are two hours or less—that makes it simple to keep track of the details and threads we'll follow.

The movies we're going to examine are available at most any video rental store. Though current DVD technology allows you to quickly find any exact scene to replay again and again, you don't need the most current technology to make use of the lessons in this book, since we aren't going to watch the movies in pieces or scene by scene.

Watch each movie as a whole, beginning to end. Then read the chapter. You may want to go back and watch a particular scene again, but it won't be crucial to understanding a chapter's lesson.

The most wonderful stories are magical because traces of characterization weave together seamlessly with the plot, foreshadowing, and all the other parts that make up a story. Don't be surprised when conflict is mentioned in the chapter on characterization, or a plot element sneaks into the discussion on motivation and character growth. A well-crafted story should make it difficult to distinguish one element from the other. That's the kind of storytelling you want to do, isn't it? Complete. Whole. That's the goal.

THE DIFFERENCES

There are things about writing fiction that we won't try to learn from watching movies, because they are handled differently in the two forms.

BEGINNINGS

Beginnings, for example. Movies often start with a character driving to some new location or showing a character in his or her youth. There might even be flashbacks to another time and place. The opening credits often appear over early scenes as we get a general overview of a character's life, where he's been if it's important, or where he is now (**Harry Potter and the Sorcerer's Stone**, for example). You, the storyteller, have to establish a normal before you can show how this character's life is going to change. Showing the normal is just different in most movies than it is in books.

Other movies, especially those in the action and suspense genres, begin with the back-or pre-story that puts the action in motion (**True Lies**). Important details are established. Then ten percent of the way into any movie—according to Michael Hauge, renowned author of *Writing Screenplays that Sell*—an opportunity is presented to the protaganist, and the foward movement of the story begins. It's amazingly consistent. Time it for yourself. You'll find it fascinating. The first ten minutes of most movies are a kind of "information dump" that few novel readers would tolerate. That kind of beginning would be the kiss of death in a book. You wouldn't want to start reading with a complete summary of your main character's life until now. Without the accompanying visual images to draw the reader in, you wouldn't want flashbacks to another time and place. You'd want to sprinkle background details into your story sparingly and along the way. Not all at once, right up front.

No one—not an editor, not an agent, so definitely not a stranger who has to plunk down money to read your book—no one except maybe family and really close friends will read past the first page if you start your book that way. Books often start with the action in progress . . . already ten minutes into the movie, if you will.

BACKSTORY

Slipping background information into a book is more complicated. The writer reveals things as they're needed, and readers discover those pieces, here, there, and everywhere. It's like putting together a puzzle. Sometimes it's a challenge for the writer to get those bits and pieces in without resorting to awkward information dumps. We've all read books where a character tells her mother important details any decent mother would know, (like where the character currently lives).

Though screenwriters may have less of a problem figuring out how to put backstory or a character's background in, authors have a huge advantage over screenwriters in another area: a character's point of view.

POINT OF VIEW

Unless you write from a God-like omniscient point of view—which wasn't fashionable or wise until the popularity of *Harry Potter* novels brought it back into limited style—most information in a novel comes directly from the characters' thoughts and actions. Movie audiences can't experience and share a character's thoughts and perceptions without the occasional voice-over.

That's the reason readers rarely find watching a movie as emotionally satisfying as reading the book it was based on. We get more emotionally involved when we feel a story from a character's point of view.

That intimacy, that direct insight into the character's mind, makes reading friendly. Very personal. Being in a character's head watching the story unfold through his eyes, hearing the character's thoughts brings the reader very close to the character. The character's defeats or victories feel personal. His joys and heartbreaks become yours, too. It's impossible not to feel that you, personally, have something at stake when you begin to know a character from the inside out. When you see the whole world through someone else's eyes, think his thoughts, dream his dreams, experience his expectations and disappointments, you come to know that character better than you know your own mother. (At least, I don't know anyone who shares their mother's thoughts. Do you?)

In a movie the audience has only the camera's point of view. A camera is a cold, impersonal thing. Movie characters come to "life" because real people bring them to life. We see them in flesh and blood and living color up there on the screen. Actors provide depth and insight into the character by reacting with facial expressions and body language. But an actor might be one person today and someone totally different in a movie out next month. We eventually come to see *Big Name Actor* playing "character X" instead of being "character X" because the next month we see the same actor playing "character Y." That makes it harder to get close to characters in movies.

WATCHING VS. READING

The last major difference between how books and movies tell stories is the way the audience interacts.

People watch movies in a crowd of strangers. The reaction of the audience in a theater is usually contagious. (If you don't believe me, watch any of the *Harry Potter* movies with a passel of preteens, then watch it with a middle-aged audience. I guarantee you a totally different experience.)

Reading a book is private and personal. A writer depends on carefully chosen words to create a mood or set a tone that keeps the reader reacting (and feeling) the way the writer wants him to react.

In the actual writing, a screenwriter expects and gets a whole army of help to tell his story. Sometimes, the screenwriter is working from a novel or book, therefore basing his version on some other writer's story. It isn't unusual for a studio to have a whole team of writers working on a script. They might bring in another team or a story doctor to revise it again. Often they have different writers rewriting dialogue for scenes, even as they are filming. All of those writers have an effect on what we eventually see on the screen. (Though I've heard it isn't unusual to have ten or even twenty different writers who have worked on a screenplay or script, when I name names throughout the rest of the book, I will be using only the names of the screenwriters who are listed when the credits roll in the film.) After the writers finish, actors, directors, cameramen, set and costume designers, and a wide variety of others serve up their combined notion of how the story looks. The story we finally see is a conglomeration of all those visions.

A novelist doesn't have go-betweens. Though an editor may help fine-tune the work, what passes from the storyteller's head directly into an anonymous reader's brain are the writer's words and thoughts. An author provides details and word pictures to assist the reader in "seeing" the scene, but the final vision is up to the reader's imagination.

Those are some of the differences between storytelling in movies versus books, but a trip to the bookstore will quickly show you the similarities. In the chapters on premise, plotting, and other tricks of the trade, we'll explore some of those similarities. Both **Jaws** and **Bridget Jones's Diary** are direct adaptations from books. **Bridget Jones's Diary** and **Clueless** are updates of Jane Austen's classic novels, *Pride and Prejudice* and *Emma*. We'll compare some book scenes with corresponding scenes from the movies they became. You'll quickly understand why books can become movies and movies can become books.

Movies are stories. They start the same place a book does: as an idea in a writer's head. They even evolve the same way: from a blank sheet of paper to a bunch of pages with words strung together to make a story. A well-told movie has most of the same elements of a well-written book. And those common elements are what we're going to study.

The assigned movies and the subjects we will study include:

While You Were Sleeping . . . . .Characterization

Spider-man .External Goals

Speed . . . . .Internal Goals and Character Growth

Clueless . . . . .Premise

Lethal Weapon . . . . .Creating Tension

The Sixth Sense . . . . .Conflict

Die Hard . . . . .Suspending Disbelief

Bridget Jones's Diary . . . . .Plotting

Jaws . . . . .Putting It All Together and Other Tricks of the Trade

WATCHING MOVIES WITH A WRITER'S EYE

Do watch the movie assigned at the beginning of each chapter before reading the chapter, even if you've seen it ten times. If you don't watch it again, you'll be cheating yourself. To really take in some of the nitpicky details we'll discuss, it should be fresh in your mind. If you haven't seen one of the movies—or if it's been a while—you'll want to watch it twice. Once for enjoyment. The second time, watch with a writer's eye.

Watch the movie thinking about the chapter topic. Take notes. Find the scenes that show characterization or conflict or whatever the topic is. When you get around to reading the chapter, give yourself points for being right.

Watch for elements in the movie that do *Double Duty.* Every word and sentence of your manuscript must be there for a purpose. It should show characterization and advance the plot or show motivation, for example. Most writers strive to do more than one of these things with a sentence or line of dialogue. Perhaps because the format restricts the time they have to tell a story, screenwriters are especially adept at achieving that goal with a line of dialogue or a snippet of a scene. Recognizing the things that do *double duty* in a movie will hone your skills for doing it yourself. In the following chapters I will note and name some of the things that do *double duty* to help you hone these skills.

Watch body language. According to the people who research this kind of thing, nonverbal communication accounts for more than half of what we "hear" from someone else.

It's absolutely mind-boggling what our intellect can see and understand in milliseconds. *Blink: The Power of Thinking without Thinking* by Malcolm Gladwell is a fascinating book on the subject. Gladwell makes the point that our first impressions aren't accurate. But he also tells us that when they go awry, it is for very specific and consistent reasons. The book explains those reasons and shows how to identify and understand them.

Actors try to convey what their character is thinking or feeling with body language. Unlike the rest of us in our normal everyday lives, they have nothing to hide. In fact, the better they do it, the more success they find in their careers. And we, the audience, have every reason in the world to interpret them the way the actor intends us to.

Fiction writers have to express with words what actors do by simply raising an eyebrow, turning their back on someone, or suppressing a smile. Amazingly, an accurate description of a nonverbal communication conveys a message almost as clearly as seeing the same expression would. As you watch the movies, do you see a certain feeling conveyed perfectly with a subtle facial expression? Jot down a description. Try to nail what's different about this particular expression. What keeps it from being just like any other? Capture body language in a few brief words, and your reader will sense things about your characters that it would take you paragraphs and pages to tell in any other way.

Watch for ways to use all five senses. Movies effectively use only two senses: sight and sound. Good books use all of them—sight, sound, touch, taste, and smell. Watch for things in movies you could translate to smell, taste, and touch in a book: the sweetly acrid smell of spaghetti sauce burning in the apartment next door; the mellow, yet slightly bitter taste of rich dark chocolate; the rough yet comforting feel of the fleece throw that your heroine pulls over her as she curls up on the couch to lick her wounds. Your written descriptions, using all five of the senses, can be just as graphically intense as the sights and sounds of movies. They can make a stronger impact because you can get inside the character's head. You can translate those sensations—and the way they make her feel—to the reader.

Watch what the camera tells you. If the camera comes back to or focuses on a particular object, why? If it's a subtle thing, something you wouldn't have noticed if you weren't watching with a writer's eye, what's the significance? What does it mean? If you were writing the scene, which character's perspective would the reader have to be in for that particular item to have meaning? Whose point of view would put the most effective slant on what happens in this scene? That's great practice for deciding which point of view will be the strongest to tell which parts of your stories.

Analyze the settings. The camera tells you lots of other things. Where or when does the movie take place? Why? Is there a logical reason the screenwriter chose this? What about specific scenes? Was this setting convenient and cheap (within the movie budget), or does it do *double duty* in some way? *Spider-man* would have required minor story changes if it weren't set in New York City, but it realistically could take place in any city. *Jaws* had to happen by an ocean. *A Christmas Carol* wouldn't have been a story without Christmas. *While You Were Sleeping* could have been set at any time with some changes, but Christmas made the emotions of the story stronger. Neither books nor movies always have rhyme or reason for their settings. But once in a while, you'll realize the writer (or director or set designer or whoever) built more impact into the story just by placing the story or scene in a certain season or locale. Every story has to take place in some place or time. Exercise and train your instincts to consider whether a certain season, place, occasion, or circumstance adds something to the story. Would another setting have more impact? Or less?

Analyze everything. Just as with locations and seasons, wonder *why* the director or writer or someone chose to do a particular thing in a particular way to show this story. Was it intentional and what is the impact on the story?

Watch for subtleties. In every scene where Bruce Willis couldn't make a connection with his wife in *The Sixth Sense*, something red was emphasized. Red is the traditional color for stop. Was the director trying to tell the character—or us—to stop and think about why he couldn't connect with his wife? In *Bridget Jones's Diary*, Bridget kept track of her weight, the number of cigarettes smoked, and number of drinks she had to measure her personal success . . . or lack of it. In *Under the Tuscan Sun*, sunflowers seem to be a symbol for the character's growth. First we see a single wimpy one. Then there are more and more. As the character blooms, we see a whole field of the flowers. Are there signals you can give your readers to emphasize certain points or to echo themes? Become intent on discovering small details that make big differences in the story's impact on the audience. Consider how adding a symbol, or using a metaphor or simile, can add a little more depth or subtle meaning to your story.

WHO IS YOUR AUDIENCE?

I'm assuming your target audience is the same as mine. If you only want to write for yourself, you don't need this book. Write what you want. If you want to write literary fiction, you're welcome to anything that helps, but everything here doesn't necessarily apply.

I assume you want to write popular, an-editor-will-be-interested-in-buying-it, written-for-readers stories. In other words, publishable, commercial fiction.

In using popular movies to learn story-telling skills for writing popular fiction, this book deals in generalities. For every example given, you will be able to name both movies and books that don't conform to the rules. That's good. That means when you know and understand the general rules, you, too, will understand how to break them. . . and still find markets for your work.

QUICK TIPS 👉

WILL HELP YOU TAKE THE LESSONS FROM THIS BOOK TO THE PAGE AS YOU WRITE YOUR OWN STORIES.

Few writers sit down and write a first novel without study, planning, practice, feedback, trial and error, and then more study, practice, and more practice.

And almost everyone has something that is especially difficult for him or her to grasp. Knowledge is not necessarily the same as understanding. A child may hear a word often enough to know the word, but he may not understand what "hot" means until he experiences it for himself.

I know writers who wake up in the morning knowing the plot of their next story, start to finish, with every intricacy and detail, every twist and turn along the way, fitted together perfectly. But they struggle to understand how to build characters with the proper motivation and depth to carry off their flawless plot.

Plotting has been my particular challenge, while characterization made gut-level sense from the beginning. I was delighted when one of the things I struggled with became clearer one day when I was watching a movie. That's when I began to watch them differently.

Learning how to juggle all the pieces and parts of a story, and getting them to fall in the right order in the right amounts, is part of the process of learning to write fiction. If a movie helps you find true understanding of a different story element or how something fits together, it will shorten the learning process for you.

The final stage of learning happens when we put to practical use what we've learned. I've included *Quick Tips* and *Quick Fixes* along the way to assist you in reaching that goal.

I don't know whether your protagonists are male or female so, though I've tried to be consistent chapter by chapter, I've used "he" and "she" randomly when talking about your characters. It's less clumsy than using s/he and more politically correct than discriminating against one or the other.

I've also included appendices with several forms that might help you use the things we'll cover. Besides aiding in planning and plotting your own story, the forms can be used as study guides. As you watch a movie or read a book, fill out the form that applies to the story

QUICK FIXES ➋▬▬o

ARE DESIGNED TO HELP YOU EVALUATE YOUR WRITING AND THE STORIES YOU'VE ALREADY WRITTEN, IN ORDER TO MAKE THEM STRONGER.

element you're trying to analyze (e.g. internal goals). It will help you understand how that element works when you're writing something of your own later. Since I find it maddening to have to either retype the forms found in books or tear up the book to utilize them, the forms can also be printed from my Web site: www.lightscamerafiction.com. Visit me there on occasion, and you'll find additional articles and tips that may also be helpful.

Finally, you should know that, except in places where I profess otherwise, I can't begin to know what a specific author or screenwriter was thinking or not thinking when she or he was writing some of the movies and books we'll discuss. I guess—based on my own experiences and conversations I've had with other writers. If the truth be known, much of the thinking that goes into writing a story happens before the writer has put a single word on the page. Once the actual writing starts, much of the thought goes on at some subconscious level, especially if the writing is going well. So even an author may not be able to tell you what he was thinking at the time he wrote a certain scene.

There's a zone where writers go—similar, I suspect to the zone you hear athletes talk about—where the story takes over, and suddenly, it's two hours or five hours later, and you have no idea where the time has gone, let alone what you were thinking during that time.

Several years ago I watched a biography about Mary Shelley on TV. She, her husband (the poet Percy B. Shelley), and some friends, including Lord Byron, were staying in the area where *Frankenstein* is set—during what she called "a wet, ungenial summer" with incessant rain that "confined them for days." Their little group began translating German ghost stories to pass the time and finally decided they'd all write a ghost story themselves.

Mary was the last one of the four to come up with a story idea, and the first and only one to finish. (I don't remember exactly how long it took her, but I remember it was written in a blaze.) The biographers on the show then began speculating about the deep and intentionally hidden meanings in the story. (They didn't call it speculation, though. They presented it as fact and truth.)

After all that, after all those details about how it was written—in a weekend or a little more—the biographers wanted me to believe she had intentionally planned all sorts of symbolism about her father, her childhood, and all sorts of other things? I had to laugh.

No matter how great and detailed the story plan—and in Mary Shelley's case, we aren't talking about a lot of time for planning here—no one who's felt the rush of a story take over and take off, no one who's entered the zone your creativity takes you to when the words are coming that quickly—would buy the notion that Shelley planned and included layers and layers of meaning in telling the story of *Frankenstein*. That isn't how it happens.

Her subconscious may have infused underlying meaning that a thoughtful reader can discover and take away; and a writer may add subtleties during revision, but nothing will convince me she wrote this story for any other reason than to entertain herself and her friends. And that's how she herself describes what she wrote. Nightmares woke her in the middle of the night; nightmares that grew from the discussion the group had been having earlier in the evening about Dr. Darwin's experiments. She simply wrote her nightmare down.

My goal in writing this book is to show you examples that will help you understand—at a gut level—some of the elements in a story so that you can go to that writer's zone more frequently, and let your subconscious take over the heavy thinking.

Another goal is to help you leapfrog past some of the things that are difficult for you, and might deter you from starting or finishing your novel. By the time you finish reading this book, I hope you better understand some of the writing techniques and tools that would take lots of trial and error to learn by traditional methods.

By showing you things instead of telling you about them, I want you to "get" how to make your scenes do what you want them to do, how to make your stories more compelling, and your characters well-rounded, solid, and real. By showing you things instead of telling you about them, I want you to see not *how* to write your story—that art will still take practice—but how to *show* it.

I want you to have a better understanding of why some of that magic you've found in so many stories *is* magic. My fondest wish is to help you create magic of your own.

ADDITIONAL MOVIES

Though each chapter will use a specific movie to show that chapter's topic, I'll also reference or use examples from these movies (another great excuse for watching more movies and calling it work):

Aliens

Heart and Souls

Life as a House

The Shawshank Redemption

Braveheart

The Elephant Man

Big

Thelma and Louise

It's a Wonderful Life

North by Northwest

The Rock

A Christmas Carol

About a Boy

True Lies

Psycho

Dirty Harry

Killer Klowns from Outer Space

Star Wars

The Matrix

Don't Say a Word

How to Lose a Guy in 10 Days

My Cousin Vinny

Raiders of the Lost Ark

Holes

The Usual Suspects

The Sting

Harry Potter and the Sorcerer's Stone

Under the Tuscan Sun

Chapter Two

Characterization

ASSIGNMENT: *WHILE YOU WERE SLEEPING*

How do you use words to give a vivid impression of someone? Their out-ward appearance? That's easy. But how do you differentiate one tall, dark, and handsome man from the other tall, dark, and handsome men you know? How do you turn a caricature into a specific, unique, and totally human indi-vidual? That's a problem fiction writers struggle with daily.

You might say the first man is vain, the second one is intelligent, and the third one is generous, but be prepared to answer a lot of questions. Each of those descriptive words is vague, and anyone you say them to has his or her own interpretation of what those words mean. So if you want to tell me about someone who, at your first meeting, struck you as disdainful, tell me what he did to make you think that. Give me an example instead of a word. Give me a *scene* that shows him being disdainful.

In the very first scene of *Life as a House*, the screenwriter Mark Andrus, shows us that his main character is disdainful of himself, the people around him, and the world in general, before a word has been spoken.

It's morning. George (Kevin Kline) awakens. As his neighbor makes a face of disgust and her teenage daughter strains to see what she can see, George walks out of his house in his skivvies to the cliff overlooking the sea and urinates. His action leaves the solid, unforgettable impression that this character is disdainful of the world in general. Piss on it. Piss on the whole world.

You can't go wrong by opening your book with a scene, such as the one in *Life as a House*, which shows your main character's most dominant trait. (*Double Duty*: the scene also shows what this character will have to change to reach his goal.)

That's great for one scene, but how does that build a complete character? How do you show why the character is disdainful without the character telling you? How do you show not just the emotions of the moment, but also the whole person? How do you show the way he thinks? What motivates her actions? What shaped the character? In fact, how do you put the information you now know into your book?

Screenwriters have an advantage when it comes to bringing characters to life. Actors and actresses play the assigned roles and infuse some personality into the character. Granted, if the writer has given the actor wonderful dialogue and a great story, the actor's job of bringing a character to life is easier. And if the actor is wonderfully gifted, he can convey a feeling or attitude even if the

> **QUICK TIP:**
>
> SHATTER A STEREOTYPE.
>
> START WITH A STEREOTYPE—SUCH AS "TALL, DARK, AND HANDSOME."
>
> SHOW, IN YOUR INTRODUCTORY SCENES, THE CHARACTER'S THREE DISTINCT, NAMEABLE CHARACTER TRAITS—SUCH AS SKEPTICAL, COMPASSIONATE, AND HAPPY-GO-LUCKY.
>
> VOILÁ: A UNIQUE CHARACTER.

writer's words aren't chosen carefully. Even if the script is pathetic and the actor is as wooden as a walking, talking tree, it's hard for the audience not to see a "well-rounded" character when a living, breathing, real-life person is walking around on-screen.

Novelists don't have those solid images to give their characters substance. The people in their story come to life only when the writer can illustrate who they are on paper. For most writers that means spending some time planning their fictional folks and getting to know them better than they know themselves.

Writers tend to study the people around them, but unless you happen to live or work with someone "heroic"—and that doesn't mean in the Superman sense—you probably won't want to use your friends and neighbors as major characters in your books.

IS YOUR HERO HEROIC?

Editors describe the characters they want to read about as larger-than-life. No one would question whether Mel Gibson's William Wallace, in the movie **Braveheart**, fits that description. He's a character worth writing about because he's *an uncommon man in a common situation.* (Some might question calling Scotland's fight for freedom from English rule a common situation. But consider how long English rule lasted and the cast of thousands of common men who *didn't* fight until they had William Wallace to lead them. The murder of his wife and his desire to avenge her death changed him from being like the common men around him into an uncommon man who began to change the common situation for that specific place and time—tolerance of an occupying army—into a fight for freedom.)

QUICK FIX: ⚙

IS YOUR HERO HEROIC? TEST HIM!

HOW IS YOUR CHARACTER ORDINARY
OR EXTRAORDINARY?

HOW IS HIS SITUATION ORDINARY OR
EXTRAORDINARY?

IF YOU CAN'T SAY SPECIFICALLY
WHAT MAKES HIM OR HIS SITUATION
SPECIAL, UNIQUE, OR NOTABLE, YOU
PROBABLY WON'T CONVINCE ANYONE
ELSE HE'S HEROIC AND WORTH WRITING
ABOUT. ADD AN EXTRAORDINARY ELE-
MENT TO HIM OR THE SITUATION TO
MAKE YOUR STORY UNIQUE, NOTABLE,
AND SPECIAL.

Since most books and movies aren't about such true heroic figures, the other option is to put *a common man in an uncommon situation*. Red (Morgan Freeman) and Andy (Tim Robbins) in *The Shawshank Redemption* provide two prime examples of characters worth writing about because they are common men in uncommon situations. Andy is in Shawshank Prison because someone murdered his wife and her lover, and he was convicted of it.

Though technically the story is about Andy—a common man and his heroic efforts to deal with his uncommon situation—Red also becomes larger-than-life and heroic as he faces an uncommon situation of his own. Red is in prison because he made an irrevocable mistake in his youth: he murdered someone. He's been at Shawshank long enough that prison has become his common situation now. When he's released from prison after spending most of his life behind bars, the real world—what the rest of us would consider common—becomes his uncommon situation. He learns the priceless value of hope from Andy.

Since you've just watched *While You Were Sleeping*, you decide: Which type of character is Lucy? Is she common or uncommon? She was definitely worth writing about.

Once you know your characters are worth writing about, how do you make them come alive? Characters come to life in three stages:

The Establishment Stage

The Introductory Stage

The Proving Stage

THE ESTABLISHMENT STAGE: IT'S ALL IN THE WRITER'S MIND

For some writers planning a character means completing a fill-in-the-blank form covering every physical, mental, and psychological aspect of their character. Other writers interview their characters or give them a Meyers-Briggs personality test. Some writers start with a cardboard character based on birth order or astrological sign or some other personality stereotype. They expand from there until they have developed a unique person. These and many other practices are legitimate and practical techniques for getting to know the people who are going to be in your story. It doesn't take many projects to find what works best for you.

Eventually, most writers do the pre-work mentally or write a character sketch that hits the important points.

If you are working on your first couple of projects, the character form is a great place to start. (The one I've developed to help me discover the things most useful to me is Appendix A—on page 227.) Spend the time it takes to fill out a form for each of your major characters. Add more blanks for items you need or want to know. If nothing else, a character form will help you discover what you need to know about your characters in order for them to come alive in your mind. If they aren't real to you, they won't be for your reader.

It doesn't take much experience writing to realize that physical traits—like tall, dark, and handsome—are mostly window dressing and often the least important details about your story people. It only matters if a specific physical attribute has a powerful impact on either the character himself or the people he deals with throughout the story. (*The Elephant Man* and *Big* are movies where outward appearance is crucial to the story.) At some point you do have to decide those things, so go ahead and decide first what physical characteristics your people are going to have.

The rest of the character form is much more important. Figuring out who, what, when, where, and how this character became who he is at this point in his life will take some time. But it's time well spent. It's the foundation for your characters, and, like any good foundation, it provides a solid place to build, even though most of it won't be seen.

Before I can write a thing, I have to know my character's two or three most significant character traits. (This is the section labeled "The Present" on the Character Worksheet—Appendix A—on page 230) If I had built the characters in *While You Were Sleeping*, I would have listed Lucy Moderatz's motivating character traits as:

Lonely

Passive dreamer

Feels like a nonentity

Now that you've done the pre-work and know everything from eye color to major and minor character traits and goals for your characters, the challenge is translating that vision to paper. A written character sketch will get you started. This is often where more experienced writers start their planning.

Lucy's the protagonist or main character. If you were writing this story as a novel, most of the scenes would best be written from her point of view. Why? Because it's her story, and she has the most to gain or lose.

A character sketch screenwriters Daniel G. Sullivan and Fredric Lebow wrote for Lucy's character in *While You Were Sleeping* might look like this:

1. Lucy grew up in Wisconsin, the much-loved, only child of a widower. Her mother died when Lucy was young. Because he had to be both parents to Lucy, her father attempted to spend twice as much time with her as most fathers spent with their children.

2. By the time Lucy was seven, she doted on her father almost as much as he doted on her. He collected maps and romanticized about far away places, pointing them out on the globe that he had given Lucy's mother early in their relationship.

3. Except for her extremely close relationship with her father, Lucy's growing up years were typical of her Midwestern background. She had boyfriends, but none were serious. She participated in a wide range of junior high and high school activities, but didn't especially excel at any. She had a variety of part-time jobs after school, but tried not to work weekends because that's when she and her father would take little jaunts to places of interest within driving distance.

4. When her father became sick, Lucy quit college because the funds were needed to cover his medical expenses. They moved to Chicago where he received treatment for his illness. Before he died Lucy devoted every minute she wasn't working at her moderately paying job to taking care of him. She didn't regret a minute. She'd do it all again—plus some—if she could have him back for a little while. She hasn't gone a day since his death without missing him.

5. Dreams of exotic make Lucy feel close to her father, but it doesn't take away the almost unbearable loneliness she sometimes feels.

6. Eventually Lucy plans to go back to school, but for now she keeps her bills paid with little to spare. Besides, she has no idea what she wants to study. Maybe foreign places or languages? If she ever gets ahead financially, she'll travel, see some of the distant places her father talked about.

7. She's considered going back to Wisconsin to be among the people she's known most of her life. She's afraid that would be torture because of all the memories.

8. Lucy is a dyed-in-the-wool romantic. How could she not be, considering her father? She dreams of finding someone who will "give her the world" like her father gave it to her mother.

In that character sketch you'll find the motivation for and more evidence of the qualities we listed on the Character Worksheet. (Loneliness: paragraphs 3, 4, and 5. Passive dreamer: paragraphs 2, 5, 6, 7, and 8. She *used* to be important to someone: paragraphs 1, 2, and 3.)

The more experience you have in planning characters, the less you'll need to plan them on paper because the character really takes shape in the writer's mind. But eventually you do have to get that character on paper—to introduce him to the reader.

THE INTRODUCTORY STAGE:
GETTING YOUR CHARACTER ON PAPER

Introducing your character is like introducing a new friend to another good friend. You want the other friend—your reader—to really like or at the very least understand this new person you are introducing him to.

At the beginning of the movie, through images of her childhood and a voice-over, we're introduced to Lucy as a child with her father, going places, doing things. We see how her father greatly romanticizes his relationship with her mother. We see what shaped Lucy and made her who she is. We see that Lucy is accustomed to being very important to someone, the center of his universe. Her father does things that reveal it. Though her family was very small, we come to understand why family is a high priority to her.

You wouldn't want to start your novel here. Without the accompanying visual images that draw an audience in, you would want to start your book with action that puts the plot in motion. The subtle things we pick up in these very first scenes are things you would want to reveal later in your story.

Lucy's childhood lifestyle evaporates, the rosy glow (actually it's kind of orange) goes with it, and we're abruptly brought into Lucy's current world, the cold metallic gray of winter in Chicago. Chances are this is where you'd want to start your story.

Sullivan and Lebow give perfect examples of how to build a well-rounded character with individual scenes. We'd have recognized Lucy as real, even if Sandra Bullock hadn't brought her to life for us.

Lucy the grown-up is introduced to us in scenes that show her character traits. Right off the bat we see Lucy obsessing about a guy who comes through her turnstile each day. He never notices her, yet she imagines him falling in love with her. She *knows* she is going to marry him. We see that she's a dreamer.

The same scene reveals that Lucy is passive in her dreaming. Though he never notices her—is, in fact, oblivious to her—day after day, she also doesn't do anything to capture his attention. She just watches him and sighs.

Passively dreaming is easier and less risky than actively doing anything to make her dreams come true. This part of her personality also explains why, even though you don't see it in the story, she hasn't made changes in her life since her father died. Why didn't she go back to Wisconsin or start back to college or do something different since her father's death changed everything? Jack highlights this trait when he points out later that she doesn't have any stamps in her passport.

In this very short scene we see another important thing: Lucy is a non-entity, almost invisible to those around her. The character Peter (played by Peter Gallagher) doesn't see her as he passes through her tollbooth every day. Later we'll see an echo of this in scenes such as the one with a hotdog vendor who has no idea what her "usual" is, even though he easily remembers her boss's.

The next few scenes give us the most important insight into Lucy's character. Lucy does things alone that would normally be done with family or friends. She breaks a window trying to get her Christmas tree into her apartment.

She gives a present to her landlord, who admits with a guilt-ridden grimace that he hasn't done his shopping yet. His response translates to "I wasn't planning on getting a present for you." The audience is left to wonder if the only names on Lucy's Christmas list are people we'd consider casual acquaintances. (*Double Duty*: the scene again emphasizes the invisible/nonentity aspect of her character.)

She talks to Meow, the cat, her only family, as she decorates her Christmas tree . . . alone.

The boss guilts her into working Christmas day (though it isn't her turn) in place of others, since they have families and she doesn't. (In a book, this would be one opportunity to put in a little of her backstory since you wouldn't use it at the beginning.) We see her look longingly at the family that comes through her booth on Christmas day. We understand the most powerful force in her life right now, the thing that will guide most of her actions, her major motivating force for what lies ahead, is *loneliness*.

By the time Lucy dips her cookie in her cat's milk dish, and then pops the cookie in her mouth without so much as a thought, the audience groans. But we realize, consciously or not, that Meow is Lucy's closestcompanion and only family. And we, the audience, would feel a profound sense of loneliness for Lucy even without hearing the word. We have total empathy for her. We understand exactly why she makes some unwise, snap decisions to ease that loneliness.

QUICK TIP:

QUANTIFY THE CHARACTERISTIC.

IF THE CHARACTER IS GREEDY, SHOW THE STRENGTH OR DEGREE OF THAT CHARACTERISTIC.

WILL HE LIE, CHEAT, STEAL TO FEED HIS GREED? WILL HE GO AS FAR AS MURDER? SHOW HOW FAR A PARTICULAR CHARACTER TRAIT WILL TAKE THIS CHARACTER IN HIS ATTEMPTS TO REACH HIS GOALS.

That—the small act of dipping an Oreo in a cat's milk—is the show-don't-tell every writer strives to achieve when establishing fictional characters.

We've also learned that Lucy's loneliness doesn't lead to desperation. Lucy's loneliness is quantified in the scene with her landlord when we find that, no matter how lonely she is, she isn't interested in Joe Jr.

The screenwriters did one final thing while establishing Lucy's character: they made her universal by giving her emotions everyone can identify with and understand. Lucy talks about her dad with fondness; everyone can understand fondness for a father. She misses him; everyone can understand and sympathize with her grief and loneliness. Those universal feelings help the audience establish a bond with Lucy—something you must do with readers if you want them to continue reading. (We'll get into the Universal Language of emotions more in the chapter on Creating Tension.)

QUICK FIX:

FIX A FLAT CHARACTER.

IF THE CHARACTER ISN'T COMING ALIVE AND FEELING REAL TO YOU YET, DOUBLE CHECK:

DID YOU GIVE THE CHARACTER AT LEAST ONE TRAIT OR MOTIVATING EMOTION EVERYONE HAS EXPERIENCED AND ANYONE CAN IDENTIFY WITH?

Lebow and Sullivan gave us an added bonus in Lucy. They let her deal with her grief and loneliness without whining, without self-pity, and with her sense of humor intact. In doing so they gave us what Jack describes as a "really, really likeable" character. That makes it easy to root for her, even when later she does a few less-than-admirable things.

Through these active opening scenes, we've learned about Lucy's emotional, internal, private self. We see her current state of affairs and understand how she wants things to be in the future. (*Double Duty*: her goals are established.)

Without verbalizing or even hinting at the words we've listed to summarize Lucy's character traits, the viewer/audience has seen the things that will motivate her and explain the way she reacts—or doesn't react—to whatever happens next. Without consciously thinking about any of the character traits the scenes have revealed, the audience understands who the character is and is ready to accept the way she will act and react to the struggles ahead of her.

Write those kinds of scenes to reveal your characters' traits in your books, and you don't have to worry about your characters being real for the reader. Then keep them true to those traits, as you maneuver them past the obstacles your story will make them face. That is the Proving Stage.

THE PROVING STAGE: OR TO THINE OWN SELF BE TRUE

After several scenes that reveal who your character is, you're ready for the last stage, the proving stage—or the rest of the book.

The only thing you really have to remember about characterization, once you've introduced your character to the audience, is Shakespeare's oft-quoted line from *Hamlet*: to thine own self be true.

Your character has to be true to the characteristics you have established for him. How do the established character traits given to Lucy predict how she will react when the story begins to throw a variety of situations at her?

In the scene that actually launches the action of the story, Lucy jumps on the tracks to save Peter. But she continues to establish herself as a passive dreamer. She pats his face, talks to him, and enjoys (briefly) her chance to be close to him. Tugging on him, patting his face, and talking to him doesn't work, so with the train boiling down the tracks toward them, she shows that she will take active control when it is absolutely crucial. (*Double Duty*: the scene foreshadows her actions at the end of the movie.) She rolls him off the tracks to save him.

When she is embraced and admired as a hero by everyone at the hospital, it's in Lucy's character to take the line of least resistance most of the time. She goes with the flow and doesn't say she is *not* Peter's fiancée. We easily accept her excuse for not coming out with the truth, because we've already seen the scenes that showed this passive part of her character. Had the screenwriters told us in the beginning that Lucy was passive—a vague word we would all interpret differently based on our own experiences—we wouldn't necessarily understand why she didn't correct the misunderstanding immediately. We accept it without question since they showed us instead.

As in life, a fictional character's actions speak much louder than words. We willfully ignore reality right along with her for another reason. Her loneliness. We want her to have this family around her for at least a little while. We're pleased that she can feel special and important again. For the moment she's no longer a nonentity.

INTRODUCING OTHER CHARACTERS

Until now Lucy knows Peter only from a distance. He is handsome and obviously successful. But it isn't until we see the man who always heroically offers his seat on the train to someone who needs it, that we finally understand what attracted Lucy to him in the first place. Lucy finally meets the real Peter through his family. So far, so good. If his family is any example, he's going to be really good (when he wakes up).

QUICK FIX: ⚒

IF A SCENE ISN'T WORKING . . .

ONE POSSIBLE CAUSE? REVIEW YOUR CHARACTER'S TRAITS. IS YOUR CHARACTER STILL ACTING AND REACTING IN A WAY THAT IS TRUE TO THOSE TRAITS?

Then she is presented with his "stuff." In a book, you'd get to hear at least some of her thoughts. Which Peter is real? The one she sees offering an old lady his seat every day, or the one carrying a bunch of vanity pictures of himself? What does it say about a person whose family believes he is engaged, but he hasn't had the time to tell them? What kind of person has this wonderful family and then mostly ignores them?

By the end of the movie—even though we know in our heart and soul that everything is going to end up happily ever after—Lucy has stayed true to the character the writers established for her every step of the way. So we're on the edge of our seats as she walks down the aisle to marry Peter. Will Lucy quit being passive long enough to bring about a satisfactory resolution? She's the only one who can—by 'fessing up.

Confession goes against every need-to-be-important-to-someone, lonely, passive dreamer instinct in her. In doing so, the man who "gave her the world," Jack, the Protector, will probably never forgive her. She'll lose the friendship and affection she's gained from the family who has eased her loneliness and made her feel important again. She'll have to give up exactly what she dreams of: love and a family. But to set things right, she'll have to take active control instead of going with the flow. She's proven already that she *can* take active control in an emergency. (*Double Duty*: character growth and internal conflict.)

NEWTON'S LAW

Writers have adopted a scientific rule to use for their own purposes: Isaac Newton's "for every action, there is an equal and opposite reaction." It's a handy rule for keeping characters true to themselves.

The rule is useful in a myriad of ways, but applying it to characters—while you consider their character traits and background—produces real people.

Say you have one person taking a shower and another person who walks in on that character. (That's the action.) Each character in the situation will react. Their reaction will be based on their background and character traits.

Let's take the person in the shower first. If it's a four-year-old child, not yet aware that there is such a thing as modesty, his reaction will be based on the person walking in. If it's his mother, he's likely to start a conversation or ask for help. He will not be indignant or surprised.

If it's a grown man visiting his parents' home, he might turn away or say, "Hey, I'm taking a shower here."

If it's an extremely modest woman—an only child who's never had brothers and sisters—visiting friends, she'll probably scream "Eek!",

QUICK FIX:

THE HIGHLIGHTER METHOD

IF YOU AREN'T CERTAIN YOUR CHARACTERS ARE ACTING AND REACTING PROPERLY, HIGHLIGHT ONE CHARACTER'S ACTIONS AND REACTIONS IN ONE COLOR, HIGHLIGHT ANOTHER CHARACTER'S ACTIONS AND REACTIONS IN A DIFFERENT COLOR. A STRIPED CHAPTER OR MANUSCRIPT WILL HELP YOU SEE BALANCE. CHECK TO BE SURE THE ACTION/REACTION IS IN CHARACTER BY APPLYING EACH CHARACTER'S ESTABLISHED TRAITS. LAST, MAKE SURE THE REACTION IS EQUAL TO THE ACTION.

turn bright red, and try to wrap the shower curtain around her. Later she might be embarrassed and reluctant to come out of the bathroom and face the interloper.

The person who entered will react based on the same criteria: Who is this person, and what are his or her character traits and background.

The grown man's mother in the example above is probably going to say, "Oops! Sorry!" and close the door.

Say a bold young man's sister and her friend are visiting him in his apartment, and he's very attracted to the friend. If *she's* in the shower, he might just hesitate a little longer than necessary before he apologizes and closes the door.

See how the reaction totally depends on the character?

Characters react to the big things and the little things. Early on their reactions *reveal* their character traits. Later in the story, as long as the characters stay true to themselves, their reactions show them being true to themselves. And as long as that happens, the reactions confirm the audience's perceptions, predict to a certain extent what they will do, show them changing, and move the story forward. Because their reaction is an action in itself, the other characters in the story have to react to those actions.

In the scene where Lucy gets a continual string of visitors to her apartment, she reacts in true Lucy fashion.

Joe Jr. arrives (Action). She reacts with tolerant sarcasm in her own put-up-with-him style. When Sol arrives (Action), she stuffs Joe Jr. in the closet because it's easier than introducing or explaining him (Reaction). When Jack arrives (Action) with his parents' engagement present, she goes with him to deliver it to Peter's apartment because, among other considerations, once again it's easier than having to explain or deal with Joe Jr. (Reaction.)

Every one of her reactions is equal to the act that produces it. Joe Jr. is an irritating gnat. She doesn't mind arguing with him or sticking him in the closet. She respects Sol. She takes him and his admission about what he knows seriously. Jack is a real threat. Her reaction to him is bigger, equal to the threat that he represents. He's already accused her of being intimate with Joe Jr. She also has to act at least interested in what his parents are giving her as an engagement present.

Those are the big reactions. But there are lots of smaller ones. She reacts to Joe Jr's accusation that she stood him up by denying it. She reacts to Sol telling her he knows the truth with a look of surprise and then relief—it's no longer just her problem—and by telling him she's going to confess everything. She's relieved again when he assures her he'll handle it. She's delighted that she won't have to. She reacts to everything Jack does by falling in love with him. On closer acquaintance, he's the person she thought Peter was.

Now let's look at Jack's (Bill Pullman) character traits. Jack is:

Protective

Dutiful

Skeptical

When we first meet Jack, we find that he and Lucy have a common fondness for family. Though logically this should put them on the same side, Jack's love of his family does the opposite: it puts them at odds.

Jack is *dutiful*. We don't know why—and it isn't as important since this is Lucy's story. The writers give hints, but we are left to draw most of our own conclusions. He may be compensating for his brother's lack of family devotion. Because Peter has always been good at everything, Jack may still be doing the sibling rivalry thing and competing for the admiration his brother has always had. Though we don't know for certain why Jack is the kind of guy he is, it is easy to know who he is, based on the solid, concrete things we see.

At first we find out more from his absence than his presence. Jack is out dutifully taking care of the family business while his family prepares for Christmas and rushes to his brother's bedside.

Jack is taken for granted. It's a good sort of taken for granted—they depend on him, trust him, and know he will be there when they need him. His sister, Mary, finally mentions him. Only then does his mother remember that Lucy hasn't met Jack. "You'll love Jack," she promises Lucy. (*Double Duty*: foreshadowing.)

THROUGH SOMEONE ELSE'S EYES

Contrast that with what we know of Peter. Peter is self-centered, self-absorbed. How do we know that when he's lying in bed in a coma? In Peter the screenwriters present a wonderful example of how to reveal character through several other characters' eyes.

His family love and admire Peter, but they don't take anything for granted where he is concerned. We know that because they tell us so in a variety of scenes.

They believe in Lucy's engagement to him and assume they don't know about it because they haven't seen or talked to him for a while. They don't see or hear from him, except when he decides to show up.

His father thinks Peter is a bit superficial. Does he tell us that? Not in so many words. But we read between the lines as he sarcastically points out that the smile Lucy fell for is fake, and a girl with the last name of a breakfast meat, Peter's most-recently-known girlfriend, shouldn't be quite so arrogant.

His mother is so relieved to know Peter has finally found a "nice girl," we can only conclude she hasn't much appreciated his other choices.

Yet when Peter doesn't remember Lucy—and that's the only thing he doesn't remember—it is easier for his own mother to believe he has amnesia, than it is for her to consider that Lucy, a total stranger, might not be the person she professes to be. "You love her," she tells him. "You just don't remember." Can you imagine a better way to show us how disappointed a mother is in her son's usual choices?

Jack sees his older brother exactly as he is. Jack loves Peter, admires his achievements, and accepts him, complete with all his flaws and foibles. But we mostly see what Jack thinks of Peter through Jack's reactions to Lucy.

He doesn't trust her much. Since we all base initial impressions and reactions on past experiences, Jack's actions and obvious lack of trust is indicative of his thoughts. Why would Jack's instincts to protect his family rush to the fore if Jack had approved of all of Peter's previous girlfriends? Contrary to what Lucy assumes, Jack's belief that she isn't Peter's type isn't exactly an insult.

QUICK TIP:

REVEAL A CHARACTER.

IF A MAJOR CHARACTER WON'T MAKE AN IMMEDIATE ENTRANCE IN YOUR STORY, INTRODUCE AND SHOW THAT CHARACTER THROUGH ANOTHER CHARACTER'S EYES. WHO IS HE ACCORDING TO HIS MOTHER / BROTHER / LOVER / CO-WORKER / ENEMY / CHILD? SHOW HIM THROUGH ANOTHER CHARACTER'S THOUGHTS, DIALOGUE, OR REACTIONS TO SOMETHING THE MISSING CHARACTER HAS DONE.

QUICK TIP:

MAKE EACH CHARACTER'S DIALOGUE UNIQUELY THEIR OWN.

GIVE EACH CHARACTER A UNIQUE WORD OR PHRASE—A DIALOGUE TAG—THAT THEY AND THEY ALONE USE. MAYBE USE A FAVORITE EXCLAMATION OR THE CONSISTENT USE OF A CERTAIN PHRASE OR WORD (I.E., "SO," "ACTUALLY," "IN FACT," "AWESOME," "DID 'YA KNOW,") THE TAG WILL MAKE THE CHARACTER SOUND REAL—SINCE WE ALL HAVE THEM—AND SHOW THE READER WHO'S TALKING WITHOUT EXCESSIVE USE OF DIALOGUE TAGS. (I.E., JACK SAID, LUCY REPLIED, PETER ASKED.) BUT DON'T GET CARRIED AWAY.

When we finally meet Jack, he is Peter's opposite. He's the self-appointed family protector Though his parents and grandmother have accepted Lucy with open arms, Jack views her with skepticism. He hasn't heard anything about Lucy in the past. He obviously thinks he should know everything that goes on in his family, since he makes that his primary business.

Lucy is an unknown. She isn't his brother's "type." Since Peter can't introduce or explain her and his family is so taken by her, someone has to have their guard up, just in case.

We see Jack's skepticism in three scenes, one right after the other. In his first appearance on the scene, he comes to his parents' home, and Lucy is pretending to be asleep on the couch. His sister tells him who she is and his response is, "No. She's not Peter's fiancée." (His doubts about her aren't even subtle.)

Early the next morning, he's watching from the stairs when she is ready to leave. We hear his challenging, skeptical side when she says, "Hello, Jack." and he replies, "I don't remember meeting you." But he tries to give her the benefit of the doubt—after all, his family believes in her—by welcoming her to the family. Her actions and reactions aren't exactly reassuring though.

Later in church, he asks his father, "Who's this Lucy?" And to his father's reply that she's Peter's fiancée, he says, "So why was she sneaking out this morning?" Again his choice of words reveals his state of mind. Characters talk like they think. He didn't say, "Why did she leave so early?" or "Why didn't she come to church with us?" He said, "Why was she *sneaking. . . .*"

Dialogue is your best friend in revealing your characters. In as much as 90 percent of your book, especially if it's a character-driven story, the dialogue will be the character's action or reaction. When the befuddled nurse tells the family assembled around Peter's bed, "She's his fiancée," you hear a muddle of everyone's reaction . . . in dialogue. And they sound like real people, all talking over each other and at once.

Your characters must sound like real people, too.

Some writers have a knack for natural dialogue. Others have to work at it. If you're one who has to work at it, sit in a busy coffee shop and listen to the people around you. Write down what they say. Don't try for whole conversations. Just get one person's speech, then another's, and another's. Then compare what you've written with your own character's dialogue.

You'll find that people rarely call each other by name. They speak in incomplete sentences. They say a lot of "uhms" and "ahs." (Leave those out of your story!) They don't finish thoughts. They don't specify who they are addressing. They leave out words and put extras in. They drop endings.

Bad dialogue is the opposite of all that. Complete sentences. Good

QUICK TIP:

PERFORMANCE DIALOGUE

READ YOUR DIALOGUE ALOUD. BETTER YET, GET A FRIEND (OR TWO) TO HELP YOU READ IT AS CONVERSATION.

JUST THE DIALOGUE. YOU'LL QUICKLY HEAR WHETHER OR NOT IT SOUNDS NATURAL. IT REVEALS MORE IF YOU CAN JUST LISTEN.

grammar. Finished words and thoughts. And characters never interrupt each other. Good dialogue falls between how people should talk and how they really talk. Usage versus rules. Strive for the in-between.

Each character must talk like only that character could or would. Their dialogue should reveal his or her own, individual slant on the world. *While You Were Sleeping* has several terrific examples to study, especially Joe Jr.'s. Almost every time he speaks, his dialogue shows his unique perspective on the world. When he wants to describe the way Lucy looks at Jack, he tells her, "You look like you just saw your first Trans Am." Doesn't that sound just like who he is?

As soon as Jack makes his appearance, his dialogue reflects his concern that Lucy might be a threat. His word choices show his skepticism (sneaking) and then show that he has assigned himself the task of making sure she doesn't do anything to hurt his family.

WHAT WOULD MY UNIQUE CHARACTER DO?

Once you are into the Proving Stage of characterization, all you have to do is ask the questions: What would a _____ (fill-in-the-blank with your character's unique traits) character do here? How would he act or react in this situation?

In Jack's case, the question would be: What would a dutiful, protective, skeptical character do here, now, in this situation?

As he becomes fascinated with Lucy himself, he learns (incorrectly) that she's pregnant with his brother's child. Though he finds the idea repugnant, the concerned, true-to-his-character protectiveness shines through. He tries to stop her from drinking the spiked punch at a holiday party.

When Jack finally admits to himself that he's falling for Lucy, what does he do? He feels guilty, of course, and sets out to be aboveboard with his unconscious brother. He offers to win Lucy fair and square by "cutting the cards" for her. When he loses (to an unconscious man!) and suggests, "Best two out of three," we know, whether he wins or loses the next two, the battle is over. It doesn't make any difference. He is not going to be able to go against his protective and dutiful nature. He can't do something that would hurt his brother or harm his family.

Jack acts like the character the screenwriters have revealed to us, right up until the (almost) bitter end. When he brings Lucy a wedding present (giving her the world she's always dreamed of receiving) she asks, "Can you give me any reason you know why I shouldn't marry your brother?" He shows exactly how conflicted he is by his answer. (Remember when I asked you to watch body language?) He nods yes at the same time he says, "I can't." He puts protecting his family above his own wants and needs.

When Lucy interrupts the wedding to make her big confession, she puts the ball firmly back in Jack's court. Though we have some worrisome moments, we don't really question whether he will admit he loves Lucy. We have no doubts about the kind of person he is.

Should we have been surprised he didn't follow Lucy immediately after her revelations, giving us a few nervous moments? No. He acted true to his character. Though we didn't see what happened, we know his nature would have made him stay behind to make sure his brother and the rest of the family were okay. Though he's begun to extend his protective instincts to Lucy, she's broken his trust. His skeptical side would have to deal with that.

When his family is no longer at risk, we know it's only a matter of when and how. And once again, true to the character we've come to know, Jack brings his family with him to witness the happy event.

And Lucy, true to form because she wants so badly to be a part of this family, is delighted with the precious audience.

Every character has stayed true to his or her character traits, every step of the way.

While You Were Sleeping illustrates how intricately character, goals, conflict, and all the other elements of fiction writing are woven together.

The good news is that once you've established your characters and know them intimately, you don't have to think much about characterization. The character traits dictate what they will do when they come up against the obstacles your plot will throw at them.

One tall, dark, and handsome man will react differently from the other tall, dark, and handsome man in your story. Each will be a specific, unique, and totally human individual. Both will act and react logically, like the people or . . . well, *characters* you've made them to be.

Chapter Three

External Goals and Motivation

ASSIGNMENT: *SPIDER-MAN*

If you studied journalism, one of the first things you learned is the Five Ws. You have to tell the who, what, where, when, and why for your story in the very first paragraph. You need to have all of those in fiction, too, just not necessarily crammed into the opening paragraph. The *who* in your story is the main character. The *where* and *when*, obviously, are about the setting. The *why* is your character's motivation.

The *what* in a novel is your main character's goal.

If a book's protagonist or main character isn't striving to achieve some specific, nameable goal, *what* is your story about?

Tough question, isn't it? No goal, no story!

Since *what* the character wants provides the story, it also provides the resolution. Does the character get what she wants? Everything between the "what does she want?" and the "does she get it?" is the "how." *How* does your protagonist succeed or fail to get what she wants. The *how* is most of your story.

When you clearly know what your character wants, what she is striving to achieve, you are well on your way to telling your story. From that point on, you only have to throw in increasingly difficult obstacles for your character to overcome, and then show how that character acts and reacts, grows or doesn't grow enough to conquer each one. The end comes when you, the writer, show the reader whether the character gets what she wants. Though that sounds simplistic, it isn't really. If your character's goal is to buy a hot new car and she has money in the bank, if she goes to the dealership and buys one, your story will be very short. (And of little interest to anyone.) In novel-length fiction, your story will have twists, turns, and surprises along the way. She'll grow to overcome the obstacles, but once the reader discovers whether your character reaches her goal, your story is over, too.

In *Spider-man*, Peter Parker (Tobey McGuire) wants Mary Jane (Kirsten Dunst). That's the *what*. Few moviegoers would say *Spider-man* is a story about "getting the girl," though Peter himself tells us it is, in his introspective introduction at the very beginning. "Let me assure you," he says in his first line of dialogue, "this, like any story worth telling, is about a girl." And then he gets specific. "That girl," he adds as the camera turns its attention to Mary Jane, "The girl next door. Mary Jane Watson."

And as soon as the screenwriter, David Koepp, has told us Peter's goal (what the story is about), he immediately begins throwing obstacles Peter's way.

TAKE THAT, YOU CHARACTER: OBSTACLES

We instantly see the first obstacle: Peter is so low on the social totem pole, not even those in the basement level with him will let him sit with them on the bus for fear of damaging their reputations. Mary Jane, we also quickly see, is way above him. She's so secure in her own status on the social scale, that she doesn't fear any damage to that status when she insists that the driver should stop the bus for Peter.

She returns to sit with the stud in the letter jacket, Flash, and we know instantly that bridging that social gap is not going to be easy for our hero. How can he even hope she'd look at him twice when the distance between them is so vast?

Obstacle two smacks us in the face almost at the same time we see the first problem. Flash is her boyfriend. She's taken.

Though she will eventually get rid of Flash herself—he turns out to be a jerk—the overall problem doesn't go away. Her next boyfriend is Peter's best friend and roommate. The early obstacle mirrors and gives Peter practice for dealing with what is to come later.

QUICK TIP:

OBSTACLES

OBSTACLES COME IN ALL SHAPES AND SIZES.

THE CHALLENGES SHOULD INCREMENTALLY INCREASE; VARY THE SIZE, SHAPE, TYPE AND SUBSTANCE OF THE OBSTACLE TO ADD INTEREST TO YOUR STORY.

EXAMPLE: FLASH IS SOLID AND REAL AND BIG.

PETER'S SELF-CONFIDENCE—OR LACK OF IT—IS VAGUE.

FLASH DEFEATS HIMSELF, AND MJ SENDS HIM AWAY.

PETER'S SELF-CONFIDENCE TURNS OUT TO BE THE MORE SUBSTANTIAL CHALLENGE.

KEEP THINGS VARIED AND INTERESTING AND UNEXPECTED.

In the next several scenes, Peter shows us how difficult it is going to be to overcome the two initial obstacles we've seen. In a charming way—we're charmed because we see him do things we've all done that make us feel socially inept—we watch and inwardly groan for him as he waves at her when she's waving at her friends who are coming up behind him. Fortunately she doesn't even notice his faux pas. Or maybe it's unfortunate, since that reinforces that he's beneath her notice, when what he desperately wants is for her to notice him. Either way of looking at it makes the point the writers wanted to make. Peter is nearly invisible to her.

Peter can't even talk to her. He watches as Harry (James Franco), his best friend, uses information Peter gave him to score points with her. Peter finally uses his camera as an excuse to talk to her. But even then the camera is a barrier, something to separate them.

We don't realize it at the time, but when Peter gets bitten by an evolved spider, his third and most formidable obstacle to obtaining his dearest wish—his goal—comes into play. He becomes Spider-man. To the casual viewer it would seem that his becoming Spider-man is more of an asset than a hindrance. It gets Mary Jane's attention. It gets her respect. It gets him a kiss. It seems to get him at least close to what he wants.

It appears that the desire to have all of those things gives Peter the motivation he needs to fine-tune his new gift into an asset, rather than an obstacle. The first time he automatically uses this gift, it's to save her.

Which brings us to another aspect of using goals in your storytelling.

THE LONG AND THE SHORT OF IT

Besides the major, long-term goal that inspires the story you want to tell, all along the way, there are other incremental goals. There are short-term and mid-term goals. These mini-goals assist in knowing what comes next in

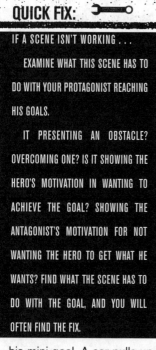

QUICK FIX:

IF A SCENE ISN'T WORKING . . . EXAMINE WHAT THIS SCENE HAS TO DO WITH YOUR PROTAGONIST REACHING HIS GOALS.

IT PRESENTING AN OBSTACLE? OVERCOMING ONE? IS IT SHOWING THE HERO'S MOTIVATION IN WANTING TO ACHIEVE THE GOAL? SHOWING THE ANTAGONIST'S MOTIVATION FOR NOT WANTING THE HERO TO GET WHAT HE WANTS? FIND WHAT THE SCENE HAS TO DO WITH THE GOAL, AND YOU WILL OFTEN FIND THE FIX.

the story.

When Peter awakens the morning after his spider bite, he notices some changes. He sees better without his glasses. He has well-defined muscles. He catches a glimpse of MJ through the window, and you can almost see his confidence grow. It's in his I-can-take-on-the-world descent of the stairs. It's in the lilt of his voice as he greets his aunt and uncle.

The short-term goal of this scene is: I'm going to get Mary Jane's attention.

An obstacle rears its ugly head: His self-confidence. We see it lag as he follows her toward the bus stop. He stops to practice talking to her. Then he is defeated in reaching his mini-goal. A car pulls up beside her and whisks her away before he has his chance. The opportunity is gone.

When we next see Peter, he's in the cafeteria, watching her progress toward him. We, the audience, are waiting to see if he will use *this* opportunity. (Getting her attention is still the goal.) We suspect he won't because, in the meantime, his earlier self-confidence has taken a few blows. He didn't make anything of the opportunity that was presented him; he didn't catch the bus. And now, he's sprouting sticky things from his hands. *Oh great*, he has to be thinking, *I'm getting weirder by the minute*. He has to see it all as something that makes him more out-of-her-stratosphere than he already is.

Then fate steps in, providing him with a chance he probably wouldn't have taken by himself. One of the effects of his transformation after the spider bite is an almost precognitive awareness of what's happening around him. He anticipates her slipping on a spill and falling in the school cafeteria.

She starts to slip. He springs into action and saves her, catching her *and* her tray of food. She compliments him on his "great reflexes." She compliments him on his eyes. He reacts to her compliments by getting tongue-tied—another self-inflicted blow to his ego. After a moment, she moves on.

He has reached his goal. He has her attention. But is it the type of attention he wants?

He notices a fork stuck to his hand. He unwittingly shoots a web and throws a lunch tray over his head. He escapes, but doesn't really escape humiliation because he drags the tray behind him. Students comment on his weirdness. (Variations of the words "freak" and "weird" are tossed out four times in this scene to emphasize what Peter already has to be thinking. It's a great example of another way to show something without using vast amounts of introspection on the part of your main character.) Later, to drive the point home, MJ tells him that he "freaked" her out.

One more note about this series of scenes: Though Peter's eventual fight with Flash doesn't do a thing to get rid of MJ's boyfriend, it does subtly show him going a long way to overcome the initial obstacle. Watch the faces of his classmates as the fight between the two of them ends. The students are all looking at him with a respect that wasn't there before. Even Harry is impressed. And MJ obviously sees him from a new perspective. So these scenes put him on a more equal footing with MJ. One obstacle down, a whole bunch more to go.

As Peter is taking out the trash, he isn't exactly feeling triumphant about getting her attention. But he does establish a better connection with her when she comes out of her house and they talk until her boyfriend, Flash, honks the horn of his flashy new car. Screaming excitedly, MJ runs to join Flash, and a new goal takes shape in Peter's head. We see it when he is perusing car ads and discovering a possible way to pay for one in the very next scene.

The car becomes an intermediate goal. He never achieves it, but getting a car doesn't really matter since the car was just a possible means to his ultimate goal—attracting Mary Jane. For now, he has two short-term goals established: he must develop his Spider-man skills and persona. Then he must defeat Bone Saw. Those are goals in and of themselves, but both are motivated by the initial, primary goal: "that girl."

You'll have noticed by now that The Goal—the long-term, what-the-story-is-about goal—provides the motivation for each short- or mid-term goal. Motivation is always the *why!* Why does he want the car? Maybe it will help him attract Mary Jane. Why does he have to beat Bone Saw? Besides staying alive—which he has to do to reach his goal—the money he'll win will help him get the car, which will maybe attract Mary Jane.

WHY, OH WHY, OH WHY?

Motivation for any goal—internal or external, long- or short-term—is what keeps the character struggling.

Why does the character want a particular goal? (Why does Peter want Mary Jane?) The *why* can be as simple as one emotional word: love, obsession, greed, hate, revenge, jealousy, as in **Spider-man.** Or it can be extremely complex. It gets complicated when the emotion can't be understood without understanding what past events led to the emotion. (See *While You Were Sleeping*.)

QUICK FIX:

IF YOUR STORY ISN'T INTENSE ENOUGH...

GIVE SOME OF THE GOALS DEADLINES. THAT INSTANTLY ADDS TO THE PRESSURE. "THERE'S A BOMB ON A BUS...."

Play the *why* game, the bane of every parent who ever had a three-year-old. In case you don't fit that category, the why is *always* about the initial goal and goes like this: Can I have a candy bar? No. Why? It will spoil your dinner? Why? You won't be hungry. Why? A candy bar will fill you up. Why? You can't grow up healthy and strong if you don't eat your dinner. Why? I love you. I want to protect you from yourself. Why? Because I said so!

Playing the *why* game with your character's goal will eventually take you the same place: the emotion. When you have found the emotion and are left with nowhere else to go, you've found the motivation for the character's deepest desire. When you want to scream, "Because I said so," you've hit bedrock.

In a character-driven story, such as *While You Were Sleeping*, the bedrock is usually deeper than it is in an action-driven story like *Spider-man*. Whether it's deep or superficial, it's important that the reader see down to bedrock, or the foundation. The motivation is the *why* for the audience, too. Knowing the *why* keeps the character from looking stupid and the reader from becoming exasperated when she doesn't give up. Motivation makes it clear why she doesn't just move on to something else.

For *While You Were Sleeping*, the simplified *why* game would go like this:

She wants to marry Peter. Why? Because she wants a family. Why? Because she's lonely. Lonely is her emotional bedrock and becomes her most important character trait. (*Why* always goes back to the original question. If it didn't, you'd end up with: Why? Because her father died. Why? He had an incurable ailment. Why? Then you'd be forcing yourself to tell a different story than the one you intended. In Lucy's case, her ultimate goal would then be to become a scientist so she could find a cure for cancer. The *why* game must stay focused on the original goal, and it ends when you find the motivating emotion.)

For **Spider-man**, the *why* game doesn't go very deep. Why does he want MJ? Because she's kind. (We see that in the bus scene.) Because she is beautiful. (That's in the eye of the beholder.) Because he thought she was an angel since she first moved in next door. (We learned that from his aunt.) Ultimately the feeling that produces the goal *is* the motivation. In Peter's case he loves Mary Jane. What produced the feeling in the first place is simply *background* or *back story*.

If the bedrock emotion will be obvious to the reader, there isn't much need to reveal a lot of backstory to explain it. For example, in **Spider-man** the audience doesn't see any reason for Peter *not* to love MJ. In **While You Were Sleeping** it isn't clear why Lucy would be so infatuated with a man she doesn't even know. The backstory becomes much more important and getting the background on the page becomes crucial.

How badly does the character want her goal? Will she kill to reach her goal? Lie, cheat, steal, betray her best friend and her mother? If the goal is a million dollars, the audience won't question too much why the character wants it. Who wouldn't want a million dollars? In that circumstance the backstory becomes less important, and this question—what will she do to get it?—becomes paramount. You, the author, must know how-far-will-she-go because that will be part of your story. The audience will find out because the obstacles you throw at the character will increase until they test the limits you've placed on her.

At what point will she give up? At what point will the prize—the goal—no longer be worth the struggle? Your story will answer these questions.

ALL FOR GOALS AND GOALS FOR ALL

You've probably noticed that Peter isn't the only character who has goals. MJ's emotional motivation may be escaping her home life, but her goal is to go to the city to become an actress. Harry, his best friend, longs for his father's respect and admiration. (A very brief scene at the beginning when Harry was introduced showed us his motivation.) Harry's father (aka the Green Goblin) wants power. Peter's uncle and aunt want nothing more than to raise Peter to be a responsible adult.

The editor at *The Globe,* where Peter is a freelance photographer, wants to "sell papers" (intermediate-term goal) so that he can to make money (long-term goal). His why is obvious—simple greed. He is selling lots of papers because he has exclusive pictures of Spider-man; but he isn't satisfied. He wants to sell even more papers so he can make lots more money. He needs a controversy (short-term goal). He is busily trying to create it, when—lo and behold—the Green Goblin shows up at the paper, looking for Spider-man and providing exactly the fuel needed to stoke the editor's controversy.

The Green Goblin wants to join forces with Spider-man. If Spider-man isn't interested, the Green Goblin plans to destroy him. Peter's very life is at risk. Peter's hard-won reputation as a hero is at risk if the editor turns Spider-man into a menace to sell papers. Mary Jane loves the hero, Spider-man. She won't be so enthralled if he's a bad guy. If either the editor or the Green Goblin gets what he wants, it's virtually impossible for Peter to get what he wants.

Suddenly two characters have goals that are in direct opposition to his. And that is the ideal in story development.

A character's goals may be good or bad. Her goals may be major or minor. The protagonist may know there's a problem or she may be unaware of how what she wants will affect others, but your story becomes instantly stronger if your character can't get what she wants, or if another character obtains what she is striving to achieve.

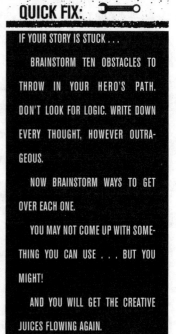

QUICK FIX:

IF YOUR STORY IS STUCK . . .

BRAINSTORM TEN OBSTACLES TO THROW IN YOUR HERO'S PATH. DON'T LOOK FOR LOGIC. WRITE DOWN EVERY THOUGHT, HOWEVER OUTRAGEOUS.

NOW BRAINSTORM WAYS TO GET OVER EACH ONE.

YOU MAY NOT COME UP WITH SOMETHING YOU CAN USE . . . BUT YOU MIGHT!

AND YOU WILL GET THE CREATIVE JUICES FLOWING AGAIN.

Though it isn't essential, knowing even a lowly walk-on character's goal will provide you with more opportunities than you might think. I'm not suggesting you spend a lot of time thinking of these in advance, but you will find it advantageous to assign them a goal when they appear.

For example, say your heroine has ordered a pizza. If the pizza delivery-man doesn't have a goal, the part of the scene where he shows up to deliver it is going to be short, sweet, and mostly unseen. Any dialogue would be an inane and boring exchange about money. Most likely it will be limited to the reader hearing the opening and closing of the door, and then seeing the heroine return with the hot and fragrant pizza. You have to resort to using a couple of the five senses to spice things up with that boring situation. Sometimes, a little bit of spice is all you need or want.

But your job as a writer is to watch for opportunities to do the things you need to do in a scene. Say your deliveryman's goal is to get a good tip. You now have the opportunity to add a bit of dialogue. "Hi, Ma'am. How ya' doing, tonight? I have a great pizza here, just like you ordered. It's hot. Let me put it on the table for you?"

With that bit of dialogue you've added possibilities. What if your heroine has had a bad day because she didn't overcome one of the obstacles you've made her face? You won't have to resort to showing your heroine's reaction to the defeat strictly through her introspection. To the delivery guy's "How ya' doing tonight?" she can respond with something that reveals her frustration. "Not so great, if you want to know the truth."

Say the heroine has something to hide, something you aren't ready to reveal yet but want to hint at. When the delivery guy offers to put it on the table for her the heroine can hastily hand the guy his money, grab the pizza, and practically slam the door in the eager and helpful young man's face. Unless you've established the heroine as a rude and brusque character, the reader might just take this as the heroine not wanting to be bothered or distracted from whatever you have her doing.

But that is the kind of subtle foreshadowing that makes readers look back and say, "I should have seen it coming. The hints were all there. The heroine didn't want the pizza guy to see what was on her table. Why didn't I pick up on it?"

Let's take the idea of using every opportunity back to the first scene on the school bus after Peter has told us his goal. If the walk-on characters—the students filling the seats on the school bus—did not have the goal of preserving their questionable reputations, the writers would not have had a chance to show Peter's lowly social status. Peter would have just taken the first available seat.

CONCRETE VS. PIE IN THE SKY

In many stories external goals are a bit more nebulous. The hero wants to help heal a troubled boy (*The Sixth Sense*). The heroine doesn't want to end up old and alone (*Bridget Jones's Diary*). These goals are not something solid and specific that you can hold in your hand.

At some points in *Spider-man*, Peter's short-term goals are also nebulous. He wants revenge for his uncle's death. Guilt motivates him. And we can understand and identify with those elements of the story. How dare the wrestling promoter not give Peter the money promised! How dare the thief kill his uncle! Revenge and guilt for not stopping the thief before he murdered his uncle give Peter the motivation he needs to reach his internal goal—but that's another chapter, the one about internal goals and character growth.

The easiest book I've written—and the one that received the most acclaim, the best reviews, and a readers' award—was my second novel. The book practically wrote itself. That, I suspect, explains some of the positive accolades I received on the book. The more consistently you can move a book forward, the more likely it is to evoke and involve a reader's emotions. Any story that connects with a reader's emotions is much more likely to make reading it a positive, entertaining experience.

Over time I've realized why that book was easier to write than some of the others: it had a definable, solid, and concrete goal. Anyone reading it could have picked that goal out. It wasn't nebulous in any way.

Pure and simple, my heroine's goal was to pay her bills. Besides eating regularly and having a roof over her head, her motivation was pride and independence. She was on her own in the big city for the first time in her life. Here are a few of the obstacles the story threw at her: she sprained her ankle—making it difficult to work; she lost her second job—the one she hoped to use to pay her electric bill, so she could get her lights turned back on; she made herself the target of revenge for some neighborhood toughs; she accepted a job to play a fake fiancée for money—and then had to overcome the obstacle of the hero perceiving that she was just after his money. It was, after all, exactly what she was after. Money had truly been her goal.

In my books with the more nebulous, idea-oriented goals, the characters did have goals.

QUICK TIP:

MAKE ESTABLISHING GOALS EASY ON YOURSELF: THINK NOUNS.

VERBS MOVE THE PLOT. VERBS CREATE THE ACTION. VERBS DRIVE THE STORY.

NOUNS CREATE A REASON FOR THE STORY.

THINK OF THE PEOPLE YOUR CHARACTERS CARE ABOUT.

THINK OF THE PLACES YOUR CHARACTERS WANT TO GO, SAVE, SEE, OR OWN.

THINK OF THE THINGS YOUR CHARACTERS CRAVE, SAVOR, OR POSSESS.

In one story the goal was to avoid loneliness over the holidays. In another my heroine's goal was to get over the guy next door. So I'm not saying you shouldn't write those kinds of books. But you should know they may be more difficult to write.

They come with built-in problems that you should think about when you're planning your book. By their very nature, nebulous, idea-type goals are more difficult to define for you and the reader.

For example try to tell someone what the movie *Thelma and Louise* was about. Initially it's about two characters wanting to escape their ordinary lives by taking a short vacation. You could actually lop off half of the sentence and just say it's about two characters wanting to escape. That comes closer to the story line, but it's a far cry from telling someone what the story is really about. *The Shawshank Redemption* gives you the same problems. What is that story about? See? Same problem.

QUICK FIX:

IF YOUR PACING SEEMS SLOW . . ..

DON'T ADD SCENES, BUT DO ADD OBSTACLES IN THE SCENES YOU ALREADY HAVE.

GIVE THE CHARACTER SOME SHORT- AND MID-TERM GOALS.

COMPLICATE AN OBSTACLE OR TWO TO MAKE IT A BIGGER CHALLENGE FOR THE CHARACTER YOU'VE ESTABLISHED.

If you have trouble defining what the story is about to yourself or a reader, imagine trying to sell it to an editor. Everyone wants to buy high concept stories. "High Concept" boils down to: Can you say what the book is about in one intriguing wham-bang sentence? It isn't difficult at all to encapsulate a story about a specific goal. *Aliens*: A small troop wants to save a distant planet from horrible creatures. *Die Hard*: A cop from New York fights terrorists in a state-of-the-art high-rise office building in L.A. to rescue hostage employees. later,

Speed was pitched simply as "*Die Hard* on a bus."

A second built-in problem with nebulous goals is that they make it more difficult to keep the story active. Action is what moves the story forward and keeps readers turning pages, but the obstacles that stand in your protagonist's way are often as nebulous as the goal itself.

For example, in my story where the heroine wanted to get over the guy next door, her obstacles were things like being forced to see him more than usual (very nebulous) because he wanted her help remaking himself to be attractive to her sister. Since the heroine liked him the way he was, her plan was to change him in ways that would make her less attracted to him. (Again, nebulous.) Nebulous obstacles tend to steer the heroine toward introspection—or doing the fighting in her head. That can make the story harder to keep active. But that doesn't mean you shouldn't write the story. It does mean you'll have to plan more carefully to keep your story moving. In writing that particular story, I concentrated on keeping her changes concrete and solid, such as making him get a professional haircut and dressing him in suits that would impress her sister. She actively looked for someone she might be attracted to. That helped keep her mini-goals physical and easily measurable. She could evaluate where she was without getting too introspective.

Whether concrete or nebulous, if a reader can clearly recognize your protagonist's goals he can understand what motivates him. Though none of us—at least no one I know—can identify with the problems of being Spider-man, we can understand Peter's desire to touch MJ's heart. We've all been there. We've all experienced trying to get close to someone, so we understand. Understanding is how a reader identifies with a character. And once that identification is there, we *care* about whether that character gets what he wants.

And that brings us to Peter's biggest obstacle: he has become Spider-man. In most stories the character changes, but he does so internally (as we'll see in the next chapter on Internal Goals). Spider-man changes externally, giving us a transparent example of how the story changes the character.

As Spider-man, Peter is a threat to those whom he loves. Anyone who wants to get to him may not be able to defeat him because of his super powers, but that person could get to him through the people he loves. They don't have superpowers. Witness the attack on Aunt May by the Green Goblin.

So, by the end of the story, Peter doesn't reach his external goal. He walks away, even though MJ is his for the taking. He proves his love for her by caring too much to put her at risk.

The good news? The ending of a story may be happy or satisfying, even if a character doesn't reach his external goal. The character may have changed her goals, as in *While You Were Sleeping*. (Lucy no longer wants Peter; she wants Jack.) Or the character may decide she doesn't want what she thought she did—*Bridget Jones's Diary*. (Being alone is preferable to being with someone who is bad for you.) Or the character may have to choose between reaching his external or his internal goal, as in *Spider-man*.

> **QUICK TIP:**
>
> YOUR GOAL: REACH FOR THE STARS.
> STRETCH. CHALLENGE YOURSELF.
> MAKE YOUR CHARACTERS DO THE SAME.
> IF YOU REACH FOR THE STARS, YOU DEFINITELY WILL NOT COME UP WITH A HANDFUL OF MUD.

A NOT-SO-QUICK TIP:

SCENE GOALS

FOR A SCENE TO EXIST, IT MUST SERVE TWO PURPOSES. EACH SCENE SHOULD SHOW CHARACTER DEVELOPMENT AND MOVE THE PLOT FORWARD.

TO SHOW CHARACTER: ESTABLISH SOME BIT OF THE CHARACTER (THE SCENE ON THE SCHOOL BUS);

SHOW THE CHARACTER ACTING TO OVERCOME AN OBSTACLE (THE FIGHT WITH FLASH);

SHOW HIM REACTING TO HIS SUCCESS (PETER'S SECRET EXCURSION TO TEST HIS NEWFOUND SKILLS AFTER THE FIGHT WITH FLASH);

SHOW HIM DEALING WITH NOT REACHING A GOAL (HIS REFUSAL TO STOP THE THIEF AFTER THE PROMOTER REFUSES TO PAY HIM AS PROMISED);

GIVE DEEPER INSIGHT INTO THE CHARACTER'S MOTIVATION (THE SCENE WITH HIS AUNT IN THE HOSPITAL WHEN SHE REMINDS PETER THAT HE THOUGHT MJ WAS AN ANGEL WHEN SHE MOVED IN NEXT DOOR);

TO MOVE THE PLOT FORWARD: SET UP A NEW OBSTACLE (THE FOOD TRAY HITTING FLASH);

DIRECTLY FACE A NEW OBSTACLE (FIGHTING FLASH);

SET A NEW SHORT- OR MID-TERM GOAL (SEEING A BUILDING ON FIRE WITH A BABY INSIDE); ACHIEVE THAT GOAL (RESCUING THE BABY);

FAIL TO ACHIEVE A GOAL (NOT CONVINCING THE *GLOBE* EDITOR THAT SPIDER-MAN ISN'T A BAD GUY).

IF YOU CAN'T IDENTIFY AT LEAST TWO THINGS YOUR SCENE DOES, YOUR GOAL SHOULD BE TO REVISE AND TINKER WITH THE SCENE UNTIL IT DOES.

Chapter Four

Internal Goals and Character Growth

ASSIGNMENT: *SPEED*

What if everyone you met called you stupid? Twenty-six times in two hours—well, three hours in real-world time, according to the timeline of the movie *Speed*. But twenty-six times is a lot, don't you think? Even if people varied the words and didn't ever actually say the word "stupid," you might start to believe you weren't very smart if you heard the variations often, right? It's enough to give anyone, even a heroic, larger-than-life, gutsy character, an inferiority complex.

Making your character feel inferior—giving him an inferiority complex—is exactly what you need to do if you want to write a story that is satisfying for the reader. Say your protagonist feels that relying on other people would make him inferior (Hugh Grant's character in *About a Boy*). The characters and actions of your story will have to prove to him that life is far superior if he does need and rely on other people.

Maybe you'll have to prove just the opposite. Your character might feel inferior because she is alone (**Bridget Jones's Diary**). You'll have to prove to her that being alone is far superior to being with the wrong person.

Maybe your character feels his irresponsibility has hurt those he loves (**Spider-man**). You'll have to prove, through your story, that the character is responsible enough to use his power wisely.

Start with a character who doesn't feel lovable enough; or independent enough; or responsible enough; or . . . intelligent enough. That's the inferiority complex Jack (Keanu Reeves) faces in the movie **Speed**. Everyone—including himself—thinks he's an idiot. And they say so to his face. Though it's subtle and

QUICK TIP:

DON'T BE SO SUBTLE.

SCREENWRITERS TEND TO BE MORE OBVIOUS ABOUT THEIR MAIN CHARACTER'S INFERIORITY COMPLEX. THEY ONLY HAVE TWO HOURS TO ESTABLISH IT AND WORK TO OVERRIDE IT. NOVELISTS TEND TO BE SUBTLER.

COPY THE SCREENWRITERS!

HIT THE PROBLEM HEAD-ON. PUT IT IN DIALOGUE. LET THE HERO THINK ABOUT IT. EXPERIMENT WITH WAYS TO SHOW WHAT YOUR CHARACTER LACKS.

YOU CAN ALWAYS TONE IT DOWN LATER IN REVISIONS.

DON'T BE SO SUBTLE THE READER HAS TO GUESS

couched in teasing terms, off-hand comments or disbelief, it is there, right out front, for anyone to see.

"You're deeply nuts," Harry, his partner (Jeff Daniels) tells him jokingly. "You're not too bright, Man, but you have big *cojones*," he is told with a certain admiration by one of the hostage bus passengers. "Are you out of your mind?" Annie (Sandra Bullock) asks with disbelief after he's done something especially gutsy. "Do not attempt to grow a brain, Jack," and "Focus, Jack, Focus." That's the sort of thing the mad bomber (Dennis Hopper) says, with a sneer in his voice, every time he talks to Jack.

When you first viewed this movie, I'll bet you didn't notice that through-out the story, Jack's partner, his boss, and almost everyone else Jack comes in contact with, insult his intelligence, time after time after time. No wonder Jack has an inferiority complex.

We get our initial confirmation that Jack believes what everyone says when, early on, Harry asks him, "What do you think?" and Jack replies, "You're the expert. I just work here." (*Double Duty*: characterization.)

> **QUICK TIP:**
>
> SUPPLY PROOF.
>
> SHOW—IN SCENES—AT LEAST THREE VALID REASONS WHY THE CHARACTER HAS AN INFERIORITY COMPLEX. YOUR CHARACTER CAN'T FIX SOMETHING IF HE DOESN'T REALIZE IT'S BROKEN.

Jack has to discover, for himself, that he is smart enough to defeat the bad guy.

The first minutes of the movie are filled with hold-your-breath action. At this point we don't think of what we're seeing as character-ization because everything moves so quickly. We see (and think) Jack and his partner, Harry, are just doing their job. They're acting and reacting to the rapidly developing situation they are thrown into. People are stuck in an elevator with a bomb attached. They are going to fall to their deaths. But the cops can't get them out, because the mad bomber will blow everything up if he doesn't get the ransom he's demanded for their lives.

But we *are* seeing Jack's character. He acts when he sees a problem. He doesn't stop to think about it. He jumps in, feet first and wholeheartedly, to solve any problem.

Just as external goals guide the story, internal goals guide the character. External goals are often obvious—something you and the reader can see, touch, feel, or at least name. Internal goals are often—though not always—

abstract. The character himself may be—and usually is—oblivious to his own internal goal. He probably will not consciously understand what it is he needs to prove or learn about himself in order to reach his external goal—in this case, Jack's ultimate goal in the movie will be to save the bus passengers and catch the bad guy. But is he intelligent enough?

When your story is finished, the audience or reader most likely will not be able to name what inner knowledge your character has gained without thinking about it for at least a moment or two.

Internal goals are what many writers call internal conflict. The concept started making sense and fell into place for me as a writer, when I began to think of it as a goal: something the character had to acquire for himself. His external goal is something he very badly wants to have; his internal goal is something he needs if he is to get what he wants.

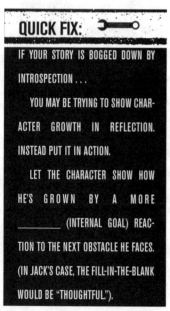

QUICK FIX:

IF YOUR STORY IS BOGGED DOWN BY INTROSPECTION . . .

YOU MAY BE TRYING TO SHOW CHARACTER GROWTH IN REFLECTION. INSTEAD PUT IT IN ACTION.

LET THE CHARACTER SHOW HOW HE'S GROWN BY A MORE _____ (INTERNAL GOAL) REACTION TO THE NEXT OBSTACLE HE FACES. (IN JACK'S CASE, THE FILL-IN-THE-BLANK WOULD BE "THOUGHTFUL").

Internal goals lead to character growth. And your main character must grow, emotionally or mentally, if you want to provide a satisfying story for your readers. As mentioned in the previous chapter, a character doesn't have to reach his external goal for a story to have a satisfactory ending. However, the main character must reach his internal goal if you want the reader to be satisfied with the ending.

The process can be compared to peeling back the petals of an artichoke to reach the heart.

PEELING THE ARTICHOKE

QUICK FIX:

IF YOUR STORY FEELS STATIC . . .

EXAMINE WHETHER YOUR CHARAC-
TER IS GROWING.

PINPOINT SCENES THAT SHOW THAT
GROWTH TO THE READER.

IF YOU CAN'T, ADD OR REVISE UNTIL
YOU CAN.

The outer petals of an artichoke are prickly and a bit tough. They are a good representation of belief the character holds. The belief restricts him and keeps him from doing something he must do to reach his goal. (Check the *Peeling the Artichoke* Worksheet, Appendix C—on page 241.)

The next couple of layers show the reader/audience what the belief is and why the hero believes it. At this point the reader assumes that the belief is true, that the character holds the belief because it is valid and legitimate.

As those layers peel away, your job is to sow seeds of doubt in the reader's mind as to whether the belief is true or not. These layers are usually successes that could be attributed to luck or the efforts of other characters or even to the character accidentally doing the right thing. During these stages the belief is so firmly held by the character that he still doesn't question its veracity.

Peeling another layer or two provides the reader with proof that what the character believes isn't true. The character has a success or two that cannot be deemed luck or attributed to someone else. Now the character questions the long-held belief. He begins to test whether it might not be true.

When we finally reach the core, he faces a final test. If he passes the test, his old belief will no longer be supported. If our character has grown, he will have conquered his inferiority complex, whatever it is.

In Jack's case, if he has grown, he will believe in and then knowingly use his brains to enhance his brawn.

JACK'S ARTICHOKE

The initial layer of Jack's artichoke is exactly what it seems: what you see is what you get. You see an experienced and "smart" cop (Harry) and a less experienced (and dumb?) one.

The screenwriter (Graham Yost) shows us two cops doing their job. Harry is obviously teaching Jack, the younger, less-experienced one. (Remember Harry's "pop quiz" in the opening of the movie? It's part of Harry's mentoring.)

Jack is obviously the less cautious, more impulsive of the two. He volunteers Harry for tasks Harry doesn't necessarily want. As soon as Jack sees a problem, he plunges in. We see that when he opens the access panel to the elevator and immediately goes in. Harry hangs back a moment, standing outside, evaluating, studying the lay of the land. And then he follows.

We peel back a layer of artichoke petals. Jack applies his mentor's earlier lesson to the current situation. He attempts to "take the hostages out of the equation" and hooks a crane to the elevator to prevent it from falling. Jack assures a dubious Harry that the crane will support the weight of the elevator. It doesn't.

We discover that Jack doesn't always test his theories or think them through. He might be a bit too impetuous and optimistic. But if everything Jack did worked out exactly like he expected it to, he (and we) wouldn't believe there was any problem with his gutsy, non-thoughtful way of doing things. (*Double Duty*: hostages hanging in an elevator *and* the crane falling, inch by inch, little by little, definitely ratchet up the suspense.) It all works out. The hostages are rescued, but Harry and Jack both acknowledge that they were "lucky."

Another layer of prickly petals is peeled away. Harry is captured by the madman. Jack still has his gun, but doesn't know what to do with it. He looks to Harry for guidance. "Shoot the hostage," Harry tells him, though he scoffed when Jack gave that answer to the "pop test" earlier—in fact, that was when he told Jack he was "deeply nuts." Harry is saved, but only because Jack acted on Harry's instructions. This layer reveals that Jack relies on Harry's guidance to know what to do. To the audience it also reveals that maybe Jack's answer wasn't as dumb as Harry suggested. Subconsciously we begin to question whether Jack is the idiot everyone seems to think he is.

The bad guy escapes, but both Harry and Jack go on to win commendations.

In a bar later, during the celebration, Jack shows that the victory has been a slight boost to his self-confidence. He verbally pats himself and them on the back with, "Yeah, we're good. We got him [the bad guy]. We won." But he looks to Harry and Lt. McMahon for assurance and confirmation. He doesn't get it. Instead, he earns a lecture about listening and luck running out. "Guts will get you so far, and then they'll get you killed. You'd better start thinking," Harry tells him, adding that he won't always be there. (*Double Duty*: foreshadowing)

He isn't there when Jack has to chase down a bus to forestall another disaster. Another couple of artichoke petals fall away as we see Jack make a lot of decisions that *seem* pretty smart. (I would never have thought to open the car door and let the speeding bus take it off so that he can get on the bus. Would you?)

It was also pretty clever of him to move all of the passengers to one side when the bus was going to careen around a tight corner, and there was a legitimate concern about the bus tipping over. It's debatable whether that tactic was effective. If they hadn't tried to counterbalance the bus, would it have made it around the corner without flipping? We'll never know but it was smart of the screenwriter. It kept Jack in character. He was reacting to the situation at hand—doing something, no matter whether it was wrong or right—instead of just letting whatever happened happen.

Jack bargains with the bomber and convinces him to let the injured bus driver get off. That seemed pretty savvy. *We* see that Jack has the smarts to defeat the villain. But it doesn't matter what we see. As the obstacles pile up, what Jack sees and feels is his inadequacy. On a subconscious level, these bright ideas play a part in Jack coming to believe he can outsmart and defeat the bad guy.

Just as with external goals and obstacles, every time your hero gets a step closer to reaching his internal goal, he hits another obstacle. In *Speed* the internal obstacles just keep coming. The obstacles are the continual drumbeat of messages from everyone else. Can he learn to trust his own intelligence if no one else does?

He's still depending on Harry when he examines the bomb under the bus. Harry is the real bomb expert, the brain. Jack is more of the muscle and the guts. Since Harry isn't on the bus and Jack is, a passenger has to relay messages back and forth between them. Jack—who is under the moving bus—tells Harry, "I can reach the wire." "No," Harry yells through their intercessory to stop him from impulsively reaching for that wire.

"Don't try any of your stunts," Lt. McMahon orders him at another point. And the bomber tells him, "Do not attempt to grow a brain." He then gives Jack instructions for delivering the ransom money and asks patronizingly, "Can you remember all of that?"

Even Jack's debatable decision to move all the passengers to one side of the bus is initiated by someone else's view of the situation. "We'll make it," he tells Annie as she views a terrifying turn ahead. "No, we won't," she says. "We will," he reassures her with all his optimism and then gets a light-bulb-going-off expression on his face as he realizes, "You're right." *Then* he makes the decision to hustle the people all to one side.

We've seen the belief (his lack of intelligence). Next, we've seen the ways he currently copes with that lack (he leaps and hopes all will be right or he trusts others to do the heavy thinking). It all reiterates, to him anyway, that he can't trust his own judgment.

An hour and twenty minutes into the movie, Jack is sticking with his dependence on others to do the thinking that will get them out of this mess. His latest attempt to save them all has backfired. He applied the guts—a ride on a dolly under the bus in an attempt to defuse the bomb—but takes Harry along, via a radio, to supply the brains and tell him what to do. Besides almost killing himself, he makes matters worse. Instead of getting rid of the bomb, he punctures the gas tank.

Then Harry identifies the bomber, and a squad goes after them. "Come on, Harry. Save my life," Jack pleads as he watches the gas gauge edge closer and closer to empty.

THE LIGHT AT THE END OF THE TUNNEL

The news that Harry—"the brains of the operation" as the bomber calls him—is dead would probably be enough to defeat Jack, if he hadn't had a little positive reinforcement along the way. (It does defeat him briefly. We see his hopelessness until Annie reminds Jack that they are all depending on him.)

But some things have gone his way. One of his gutsy, lucky suggestions—one he really had no options about—jumps them over a 50-foot gap in the highway. Then in a *thoughtful* move, he sees the sign for LAX and guides them to the airport. There they can drive around, up to speed without worrying about traffic and the other obstacles they've been facing: such as overhead helicopters relaying the exact moves of the S.W.A.T. team to news stations, and thus to the bomber's attention. That will let them focus on coming up with answers. Successes like those bolster his confidence now that he doesn't have Harry to rely on.

In his next *thoughtful* move, you can almost see his confidence grow. He realizes that Howard Payne, the bomber, is watching every move they make in some manner other than via the news cameras. That—putting two and two together and coming up with four—takes thought. No guts or glory. Just intelligence. (And another layer of petals peels away. Can he keep believing he isn't smart enough when he keeps doing things that prove otherwise?)

His next move, running a looped videotape of them for Payne to watch, is pure thought. Again, his confidence grows. Three more petals of artichoke have peeled away with each of the three thoughtful, reinforcing, successful maneuvers.

He gets everyone, including himself and Annie, off the bus. He's out-smarted the very smart bad guy and he's feeling great—momentarily.

The next several scenes show Jack flexing his mental muscles. *He's* the one who realizes that the bomber doesn't know they've been saved. *He's* the one who realizes that the bomber has already escaped with the money. We're nearing the heart. These are strokes to his battered ego. More confirmation that he *can* be wise.

GETTING TO THE HEART

But his gutsy side takes over again and Jack, once again, plunges down a hole to go after Howard Payne. Because Howard Payne has Annie. This time, shooting the hostage won't work because Howard has outsmarted Jack again. This is a serious setback to his positive gains. The mad bomber has wrapped the hostage, Annie, in the bomb. He'll blow her up if Jack does anything to save her. (He makes it pretty clear that he'll blow her up anyway when he says a bomb that doesn't go off isn't fulfilling its destiny.)

It doesn't matter what the audience thinks. It doesn't matter what Howard Payne or Annie thinks. All that matters now is what Jack thinks. He tries the guts thing first, begging Payne to take him instead of Annie. That is automatic. A character is *always* going to go to his strengths first. That's where he feels confident. And that's human nature.

Guts don't work this time. And we scrape away that last fuzzy piece of the artichoke and reach the heart. We are finally to the core of Jack's character and the story. Jack's new belief in himself has to be tested. Does Jack truly believe now that he is smart enough to defeat the very smart bad guy?

We're relieved to find that he does. We can almost see Jack's brain ticking and the proverbial lightbulb go off as he struggles with Howard Payne atop the train car. We see him struggling to grasp the bomb detonator and then holding Howard up and away from him . . . as he waits for another light projecting out into the tunnel—one like he remembers ducking earlier. So he knows it's coming. "You're so smart," Howard mocks sarcastically one last time. Then we see the light . . . and Howard is done. As Jack says, "Yeah, but I'm taller," we cheer and breathe a sigh of relief, happy that the roller coaster, edge-of-the-seat adventure is over. The threat is done. Good has conquered evil. The bad guy has been vanquished. All's well with the world.

Except Annie's still handcuffed to the bar of the train.

Jack tries his keys. He tries his usual brawn. He *thinks*, and speeds up the train to try and derail it. And then we see the courage, his real strength, the one we've come to admire. Just because he knows he has brains now doesn't mean he abandons his courage. He wraps himself around her to cushion her from whatever is going to happen. They crash . . . and survive. And again we sigh with relief and are satisfied, knowing

> **QUICK FIX:** ⚊⚒⚊
>
> IS YOUR STORY TOO PREDICTABLE? EVERY STRENGTH OR ASSET YOU GIVE YOUR CHARACTER HAS A NEGATIVE SIDE. IF YOUR CHARACTER'S STRENGTHS MAKE THINGS TOO PREDICTABLE, LET USING HIS STRENGTH BACKFIRE. FOR EXAMPLE, IF HE'S SMART, LET HIM OVERTHINK A PROBLEM AND MISS SOMETHING SIMPLE AND OBVIOUS. IF HE'S KIND, LET HIM BE *TOO* KIND AND GET HIMSELF IN HOT WATER BECAUSE OF HIS KINDNESS. ADD AN ELEMENT OF SURPRISE BY LETTING A STRENGTH BECOME A WEAKNESS. IT'LL KEEP THE READER GUESSING.

all is really right with the world this time.

What we don't consciously think about is the other reason—the reason besides the happy ending—that we're so satisfied. We're satisfied because we see that, despite everything against him, Jack has conquered his deepest fear—that he isn't smart enough. We see confirmation that we can overcome our deepest fears and feelings of inferiority.

That is why your characters absolutely *must* achieve their internal goal. So the audience can go home—or close their book with a big contented sigh—feeling optimistic and hopeful and satisfied.

Chapter Five

Premise

ASSIGNMENT: *CLUELESS*

Trying to write a story without knowing the direction it should go—what you want to say—is similar to trying to go somewhere without knowing where you're going or the details you need to get there.

Writing without direction produces pointless wandering, which is why *Clueless* is a great movie to study when thinking about premises. *Clueless* has the same premise: Life without direction leads to pointless wandering.

The movie also provides a wonderful book to compare it with so we can see the premise in literary form. Amy Heckerling based her screenplay for *Clueless* on Jane Austen's *Emma*.

A premise is a one-sentence statement that takes for granted that the statement is true. It's a theory, if you will. Your story will prove (or disprove) your theory or statement through your characters, their actions, and the results of those actions. In other words, your premise is a subtle moral of the story. That's how a premise gives your story direction.

A PREMISE GIVES YOUR STORY SHAPE

A premise provides the author with a framework for making decisions about story direction, in much the same way a map provides a traveler with a framework for making decisions about which route or mode of travel would be the best way of getting where she wants to go.

Your characters are either steadily working to prove or disprove—whichever you as the author decide—your statement. It keeps you on track.

In *While You Were Sleeping*, for example, you won't find any scenes that show how happy Lucy is that she's living a lie. You'll see her enjoying being with a family again, but you'll also see her terrified of what will happen if the truth comes out. Even when she decides to make the lie the truth by marrying Peter, she's not happy with the decision. Happiness comes when she finally tells the truth, proving the premise: Truth leads to happiness.

A PREMISE SHOWS WHAT BELONGS

The premise provides you, the storyteller, with a guide for deciding what belongs in your story and what doesn't. Say you want to write the biography of someone who inspires you. You think this person will inspire others, too. In doing your research, you find out that she owned a table that's been handed down by her family through four generations. The story of the item itself is fascinating. Does it belong in the biography? It depends.

You're writing a biography—the truth about one particular person's life. Everything the person ate at every meal in her lifetime could belong, technically, but no one would want to read the book. You have to apply the same rules to the table that you would apply to the meals the person ate at the table. Does the table have anything to do with this person's inspirational

QUICK FIX:

IF YOUR STORY IS EPISODIC . . .

THINGS THAT DON'T BELONG ARE OFTEN THE PROBLEM.

TAKE OUT A SUBPLOT OR CHARACTER OR SCENE, OR ANY ELEMENT YOU AREN'T SURE ABOUT.

(YOU DON'T HAVE TO PHYSICALLY TAKE IT OUT AT THIS POINT.) HOW DOES REMOVING IT AFFECT YOUR STORY? IF IT DOESN'T LEAVE A SERIOUS HOLE, IT DOESN'T BELONG, AND YOU SHOULD ACTUALLY REMOVE IT FROM THE STORY.

NOTE: IF A BIT OF A CHARACTER'S DIALOGUE OR A RANDOM ACTION OR REACTION LEAVES THE HOLE—NOT THE CHARACTER HIMSELF—GIVE THAT DIALOGUE, ETC., TO ANOTHER CHARACTER.

qualities? Did the meals and conversations shared around the table help shape her? Does your research show that this is one of her most treasured possessions? Does its history show something about how this person became the person she is? If so, the table should definitely stay. If not, the story of the table is a tangent you shouldn't go on, something that will detract from the story you want to tell and the inspirational points you want to make.

The same goes for scenes in your fictional story. If a scene or bit of characterization has something that leads you forward toward proving your premise, it belongs. If it's a great scene, your very best writing ever, but doesn't have anything to do with what you intend to say, it's gotta go.

A premise is valuable in that it helps you decide what is important in your story. It allows you to see what you need and what you don't.

Unlike most stories, in the movie **Speed**, you won't find a lot of scenes that show Jack's background. We see who he is, but how he became that way isn't important to the story's premise and would just slow the action down. Such scenes are unnecessary because his motivation—saving people's lives—is obvious. Backstory scenes aren't necessary because they

QUICK TIP:

START A BITS-AND-PIECES FILE...

COPY SCENES AND THINGS THAT DON'T BELONG IN YOUR STORY TO THE BITS-AND-PIECES FILE BEFORE YOU DELETE THEM FROM YOUR MANU-SCRIPT. THEY MAY FIT ELSEWHERE LATER. AND KNOWING IT IS SAVED WILL EASE THE PAIN OF HITTING THE DELETE BUTTON ON THAT BIT OF BEAUTIFUL WRITING NOW.

wouldn't do anything to help prove the premise: courage without wisdom can't defeat evil.

A PREMISE HOLDS THE ELEMENTS OF YOUR STORY TOGETHER

A premise, or theme, keeps you on track and provides connections from one scene to the next. In *Spider-man*, we see Peter's irresponsibility when he constantly misses the school bus, doesn't show up in time to help paint the kitchen, and doesn't stop the thief. We see the theme of responsibility running through almost every scene. When his friend uses his line to talk to MJ at the museum, we get the message, "you snooze, you lose." When he doesn't stop the thief, we think Peter's response to the wrestling promoter is amusing . . . until the same thief kills his uncle to steal his car. Responsibility supplies the connections between all those diverse scenes, and we get it that there are consequences of every action and inaction.

Your premise also guides any subplots you want to include in your story. Your subplot can reflect or mirror your main storyline, or it can offer a contrast to it, showing the opposite result of the actions of your main story.

The subplot with the Green Goblin in *Spider-man* provides a contrast to the premise in that the Green Goblin wants power no matter how irresponsible he has to be to get it. He proves an opposite premise: Using great power irresponsibly leads to death.

If your subplot has nothing to do with your premise, chances are good that it doesn't belong. It probably detracts more than adds. Take it out. Your readers will never notice that it's gone.

Stories that don't have a direction are the ones rejected with words like "episodic."

QUICK FIX:

IF YOUR STORY IS EPISODIC . . .
TRY TO MATCH YOUR PREMISE (OR A REVERSE IMAGE OF IT) TO EVERY CHARACTER AND SUBPLOT. TINKER UNTIL THEY FIT.

Episodic means that the story isn't a cohesive whole. The scenes read like random incidents from your characters' lives. Without any specific thing holding the scenes together, even though every scene may be in chronological order and have the same characters, you don't have one story. You have a bunch of (hopefully) entertaining scenes or possibly even a collection of short stories.

READERS NEED A PREMISE, TOO

Most readers rarely think about premise or pick it out of a book, but they need premises, too. Though readers turn to fiction for entertainment and escape—at least that is what we tell ourselves—we also read fiction (in books and movies) because life doesn't make sense. Before we had words to communicate, humans were telling stories through pictures on cave walls. Shortly after verbalization came into vogue, we began telling each other stories around the campfire. Stories are universal to every culture and time because they fulfill several basic emotional human needs.

Life is frustrating, disorderly, chaotic, and illogical. Sometimes it seems downright meaningless. We return to stories again and again because a well-written one helps provide the order, logic, and meaning life often lacks.

QUICK TIP:

THINK SYNONYMS AND ANTONYMS.

GET OUT YOUR THESAURUS. YOUR PREMISE SHOULD MOVE YOUR CHARACTER FROM ONE END OF THE SPECTRUM TO THE OTHER.

EXAMPLE: IN *CLUELESS,* CHER MOVES FROM MISGUIDED TO BEING ON COURSE.

IN JANE AUSTEN'S BOOK, *PRIDE AND PREJUDICE,* MR. DARCY MOVES FROM PRIDE TO HUMILITY.

ELIZABETH MOVES FROM PREJUDICE TO RESPECT.

A PREMISE THAT MOVES FROM ONE WORD TO ITS ANTONYM WILL PROBABLY KEEP YOU RIGHT ON TARGET.

We need to bond with other people. We need resolutions. Fiction meets both of those needs. We need to experience new things. Fiction also provides that. And one of the first and foremost of those needs is the need for completion and answers. Fiction—especially stories with a strong premise—provides that.

That's why fiction (even stories filled with fantasy and paranormal elements) must make sense, based on the world and the characters the author has created. (We'll get more into the kind of fictional sense stories need in the chapter on Suspending Disbelief—see page 135.) Characters in stories have lives that make the kind of sense readers need . . . if you have a premise.

Don't confuse a premise with a universal truth. A premise is true or false (proven or disproven) for that particular character in this particular story, not for the whole world. Just because you prove one premise in your story through your characters doesn't mean another author can't take that same premise and disprove it using different characters in a different story. A premise is not a universal truth.

A PREMISE GUIDES CHARACTERIZATION

A premise is a motivating force that decides who your characters are and what they do. (And you thought the author was that force, didn't you?) In *Clueless*, since Cher (played by Alicia Silverstone) is guided by nothing, she's motivated by whim. We see how shallow and direction-challenged she is as soon as she is center stage.

In our introduction to her, she compares herself and her friends to a Clairol commercial. She uses a computer program to view her extensive wardrobe so she can decide what to wear. She blithely compares the problems of immigration to her father's 50th birthday party.

Cher is physically, financially, and emotionally secure. She thinks she's in control of her life. But she has no real direction, no purpose. She wanders aimlessly, clueless until almost the end of the movie. Her external goal is control over her world, and she manipulates others to gain that control. Her internal goal is to learn selflessness. Moving from self-centered to selfless lets Cher grow as a character.

Josh (Paul Rudd), her former stepbrother, puts a name to Cher's lack of direction almost as soon as we meet him. He calls her a "superficial space cadet." Having no real direction, Cher hops from one thing to another, depending on what she wants to control, with little thought or regard for how her actions affect others.

In Chapter Six of *Emma*, Jane Austen describes Emma, Cher's literary equivalent, this way: "She had always wanted to do everything, and had made more progress, both in drawing and music, than many might have done with so little labour as she would ever submit to. She played and sang—and drew in almost every style; but steadiness had always been wanting; and in nothing had she approached . . . excellence."

Cher's father (Dan Hedaya) points out the *Clueless* premise when he tells

Cher that Josh knows what he wants to do and adds, "I'd like to see you have a little direction, Cher." When Cher insists she has direction, Josh quips, "to the mall!"

Frustrated when she can't negotiate her teacher into giving her a better grade—never mind that she probably doesn't *deserve* a better grade—she goes shopping to "regain her strength." What does one have to do with the other? Nothing. Again, we see her lack of direction.

She and her friend Dionne (Stacey Dash) decide to help out the teacher's personal life: He needs a good "boink-fest," Cher decides. "We should do something good for mankind or the planet," she tells Dionne. But her real objective is to soften him and make him easier to manipulate.

It works. Cher renegotiates her grade. Though Josh points out that her attempt at "making a contribution" served her own self-interest, she—and her peers—gives herself "snaps" for improving the teacher's disposition. Cher accepts their adulation and feels so good about it; she wants "to do more good."

In *Emma*, the book's namesake feels so good about the match she has made between her governess and a neighboring gentleman that she also wants to do "more good." When she begins matchmaking again, as if it is a game, Mr. Knightley, Josh's fictional counterpoint, warns her, "Better to be without sense than to misapply it as you do." Emma doesn't listen. Neither does Cher.

"Don't you want to use your popularity for a good cause?" Cher asks Dionne when Ty Fraser (Britanny Murphy) crosses their paths.

A PREMISE GUIDES THE SUBPLOTS

Ty and Travis Birkenstock (Brecken Meyer) represent a subplot in the story. The two give us an opposite image and a mirror image of the main premise.

Travis mirrors Cher because he also lacks a noticeable direction in his life. He happily accepts an award for the most number of tardies to class. He's a "slacker" and hangs out with other slackers on the grassy knoll. He talks about skateboarding, cartoon characters, and smoking dope. His attraction to Ty is instant. And the attraction is obviously mutual.

Ty reflects the opposite image. She *does* have direction. She's new in school, wants to make friends and fit in. Cher's plans for Ty fit in nicely with Ty's ultimate goal, so she goes along.

The main plot and the various subplots all flow together to eventually prove the premise. Without a premise—a guiding idea—for the story, it is much harder to tie all the pieces and parts together into a coherent whole. It would be much more difficult to keep this story, and the different characters, from going different directions. It would be easy to end with a manuscript that was a hodgepodge of episodic scenes from several different characters' lives. Working toward a premise ties it all together.

> **QUICK TIP:** 👉
>
> CARE DEEPLY.
>
> WHEN CULLING THROUGH STORY IDEAS, CHOOSE THE ONE THAT LETS YOU PROVE A PREMISE YOU TOTALLY BELIEVE AND CARE DEEPLY ABOUT. YOU DON'T GET TO BE PREACHY, BUT YOU *DO* GET TO PROVE EXACTLY WHAT YOU WANT TO PROVE THROUGH YOUR CHARACTERS. THAT WILL AUTOMATICALLY MAKE YOUR STORY MORE INTENSE AND EMOTIONAL.

That's the one reason *Clueless* isn't such a great movie to study for premise. Amy Heckerling put all of the pieces together so skillfully, it's hard to pull the puzzle apart to examine each piece. But that holds true of every good story, book or movie. It's difficult to find bad examples. Movies generally don't get made if they don't have a point. And stories that wander pointlessly don't get published.

A story that you, the author, do not believe in won't get published either. That means you should probably *believe* the premise you choose to direct your story. Can you imagine trying to write something like *It's a Wonderful Life* if you believed that no man's life had any unique or particular value? Or that one man couldn't and didn't affect the world around him? Or that success could only be measured by what you have in the bank? It would be very, very difficult, not to mention insincere.

PREMISE = INTERNAL GOAL?

You may have figured out by now that the internal goal (Cher learns to be less self-centered) in *Clueless* is often gently intertwined with the story premise (life without direction is meaningless).

In the foreword from Dean Koontz's book, *Writing Popular Fiction*, he says he doesn't address theme at all in the book because, "Theme should grow from your characters and your plot, naturally, almost subconsciously."

Writers who do not consciously use premises build them into their characters. Cher, for example, grows from being self-centered (one of her major characteristics) to being more selfless. Becoming more caring about other people gives her direction and proves the premise of the story.

That's why in the books by writers who tell you they never establish a premise, you'll find that one emerges anyway. They prove it as their characters grow and change. It's rare to find a book in which it is impossible to find the premise. Books without them don't seem to get published.

Though character growth and premise aren't the same thing, a premise usually goes hand in hand with the main character's internal goals. You won't find a clearer example of that than *Spider-man*. The premise and internal goal mesh exactly.

In the classic movie *It's a Wonderful Life*, George Bailey's (Jimmy Stewart) internal goal is to feel like a success when he's failed to reach any of his life-long external goals. He *sees* himself as a failure. The premise? Every man's life has value. At the end of the movie, George feels successful at last because he sees the value of what he *has* done, despite not having reached his goals.

A PREMISE GUIDES CHARACTER GROWTH

In *Clueless*, when Cher becomes more concerned about others and less self-centered, she finds direction and brings new meaning to her life. But she has to stumble around a bit.

Though her motives become less "self-serving"—with the teacher, Cher's goal was totally what she could get out of it: a better grade; with Ty, Cher wants to feel good about "making a contribution"—but she is still misguided. She wants things the way *she* thinks they should be. She disregards what the people she is helping want. She is still self-centered.

Things quickly fall apart because everyone won't follow automatically in the direction she wants to lead. Elton isn't interested in Ty. Ty is broken-hearted.

Emma encourages her friend, Harriet, to turn down Robert Martin's proposal, in Austen's novel, *Emma*, because she thinks the match is beneath Harriet. She thinks that Harriet should try to improve her station in life. Emma tries to match Mr. Elton with Harriet. Mr. Elton isn't interested. Harriet is brokenhearted.

Cher has to find someone new to take Elton's place in her plans for Ty's romantic life. "Searching for a boy in high school," Cher says, "is like searching for meaning in a Pauley Shore movie." Then she sees Christian, and Cher's self-interest is front and center again. Yes, she *wants* to fix Ty's life, but she's attracted to Christian herself.

When Mr. Frank Churchhill comes to visit his father, Emma sees him as a possible suitor for Harriet. But Emma's attracted to Mr. Churchhill herself. What she wants for Harriet suddenly goes by the wayside.

AND FINALLY, DIRECTION!

Things get worse until Cher finally sees the snobbery she has inadvertently taught Ty when Ty contemptuously tells Travis, "the slackers belong over there."

"I had an overwhelming sense of ickyness," Cher admits. *What did I do? I've created a monster*, she thinks. "Everything I do is wrong. It all boiled down to I was clueless (directionless)." She begins to reevaluate her life.

Emma does her own damage. She is the one who, without thought, insults someone. When Mr. Knightley points out her error, Austen reports Emma's feelings this way: "She was vexed beyond what she could think—almost beyond what she could conceal. Never had she felt so agitated, so mortified, so grieved at any circumstances in her life . . . Time did not compose her. As she reflected more, she seemed but to feel it more." Then she, too, reevaluates: "How to understand the deceptions she had been practicing on herself and living under! To understand, thoroughly understand, her own heart was the first endeavor."

Cher decides to do a makeover on her soul. "What makes someone a better person?" she wonders and discovers all of her friends have good in them, things she never saw before. She volunteers to work on the charity drive at school. She's made the first steps in her journey from self-centered to selfless and things begin to fall into place. She's found a sense of direction.

Travis is also finding new direction in his life. He's "motivated," in Cher's word. (We don't see all of the steps he takes in his efforts to find meaning in his life. We just know he has taken some when he mentions his 12-step program to Cher. This is a subplot, after all. We don't have to see every detail; we just see the reflection of the main plot. We see the aspects of it that mirror and reinforce the main premise.)

Ty quits trying to follow Cher's direction and resumes steering her own course. While reflecting the overall theme—direction—of the story, Ty proves her own premise: Someone else's direction may take you places you do not want to go.

And that subtopic ties in neatly with the subtopic of this chapter. Using what works for someone else in your writing may take you places you do not want to go.

We all have to follow our own path.

FINDING YOUR PATH

When you're just starting out, you have to find what works for you. If you've written several manuscripts but not had success selling one, you might want to try something different than you usually do on your next one. If you don't usually formulate a premise, try writing a few scenes of a new book with one. See if it makes the book stronger or easier to write. Or try discovering your premise earlier in the process than you usually do—or later. This is one of those things that each writer has to find out for himself.

I personally don't think much about theme or premise until I get to the mid-point of a book. I do limited character studies. That gives me the character's motivation (his past), his goals (his future), and the groundwork for the obstacles and challenges that he will struggle with during the story (his present). I know the character's external and—usually—the internal goal. I know the first pivotal point and *maybe* the second. But I'm not surprised if it changes by the time I get to actually writing that point in the story.

That's what I need to know to get the story started, then I hit it: the middle of the book. The going gets tough. I usually find myself floundering for days, occasionally weeks. I reread what I have. I stew. Then I discover and refine what my *premise* is, and, with a little more planning, and filling out things like the *Peeling the Artichoke* form (Appendix C—see page 238), I'm off again, racing my way to the finish because now I know the point of the story I'm telling.

Finding my premise always leads me to the rest of my story because then I have to prove it through my characters' actions. They have to figure it out for themselves. Whether the premise is obvious or subtle, it will be there. A publishable book and a good—hopefully, great—story is the desired result for any fiction writer, whatever your writing style. That means it will have a premise.

FINDING A PREMISE THAT WORKS FOR YOU

Once you understand what a premise is and how it's useful in writing your story, you need to discover a method for finding and defining it that works for you. There are multiple ways of expressing a premise. A one word theme; a more complicated "controlling idea;" a "story question", or even just a maxim or proverb.

Gary Provost—who was a well-respected writer, teacher, and seminar presenter on the subject of writing—called his premises *themes*. He encouraged saying what a story was about in one word. The example given in his book (written with Peter Rubie), *How to Tell a Story: The Secrets of Writing Captivating Tales*, is a story about Tradition. Using his model, I'd say **Spiderman** is about Responsibility; **It's a Wonderful Life** is about Success; and **Clueless** is about Direction.

In his book *The Art of Dramatic Writing*, Lajos Egris says of premise, "No idea, and no situation, was ever strong enough to carry you through to its logical conclusion without a clear-cut premise. You must have a premise—a premise which will lead you unmistakably to the goal your play (our story) hopes to reach."

Egris says premise is developed by considering what will be the end of the character in his story. He believes a good premise should begin with the primary character, suggest the conflict, and show the end of the story. So the premise for Shakespeare's *Romeo and Juliet*—in Egris's words—is "Great love defies even death." The first part is supposed to show the beginning nature of the character—Romeo and Juliet have great love; the second part—defiance—indicates how they react to the obstacles that are thrown their way by tradition and family; and the last part shows how the characters end—in death. By using this formula for *Clueless*, I come up with "Aimlessness inhibits finding direction." Does that work for you? It's awkward, but it does work for me. And it shows another thing: your premise doesn't have to be pretty.

Robert McGee, in his book *Story: Substance, Structure, Style, and the Principles of Screenwriting*, says that theme should be ". . . one clear, coherent sentence that expresses a story's irreducible meaning." He calls his story premise a Controlling Idea. I like calling it a Controlling Idea because that is exactly what a premise does for your story. It gives you control.

McKee composes a Controlling Idea (the premise) by giving the Value (in the case of *Clueless* the value is direction) plus the Cause (whether the story will end well or badly), and then adding the *why*. (Why will direction win over aimlessness?) So the controlling idea for *Clueless* would be: Purpose wins over aimlessness because a protagonist without direction finds constant trouble.

McKee's Controlling Idea shows something that's important in establishing a premise. It takes you from the vague to the specific. Anyone who writes romance, for example, might say that the premise (or theme) for their story is "love conquers all." A mystery or suspense author might want to use, "good conquers evil." Those are both too vague to be of much use. They do not give you *any* direction.

But if you start with the Controlling Idea that love (the value) conquers all (the cause or ending), then add the why (because the hero learns that to love someone else he must first love himself . . . or whatever), you have a direction that can guide your story to a satisfying conclusion.

Still others form a premise by posing a "story question." I can't tell you who, specifically, first offered this very useable method of summarizing the heart of a story. Using a story question melds the internal goal with the premise. Is Jack smart enough to outwit the very smart bad guy (*Speed*)?

Finding a maxim or quote that represents the premise you want to prove in your story is also a legitimate way of forming your story's premise.

A lot of writers simply use old sayings: A bird in the hand is worth two in the bush. A stitch in time saves nine. Seek and ye shall find. The book of Proverbs in the Bible will give you more premises than you'll have time to write, even if you live as long as Methuselah. Any of these can serve as tools to help you give your story direction.

A bird in the hand is worth two in the bush: Your character learns to value the life he has instead of envying the perfect life of his two friends.

A stitch in time saves nine: After continually making his problems worse by ignoring them and failing to act, your character learns to take action at the first sign of trouble.

Seek and ye shall find: Your character is buffeted by every whim until he finds direction.

Hmmm. That sounds a bit like *Clueless*. And that makes another point. I have no idea what premise Amy Heckerling or Jane Austen, or any of the other writers we've used as examples, actually considered as the premise when writing their stories—or even if any of them thought about it at all.

Throughout this book, I've speculated about what many authors have thought or planned or didn't plan. But my speculation is exactly that, a guess.

Sometimes not even the writer knows what she is writing when the story takes over. The real value of knowing your story premise is that it gives your subconscious something to work with.

As a writer, you are wise to use whatever gives you direction in writing your story. The reader takes his own interpretation away when he finishes.

The reader's interpretation is colored by his own life experiences, his situation, and the way he thinks. Logic and meaning may be the subconscious reason he reads, but premise doesn't concern him as long as you've given the story the shape it needs for him to enjoy it and be entertained, beginning to middle to end.

However you find your premise, however you word it or use it, premise is a wonderful tool for the author.

Chapter Six

Creating Tension

ASSIGNMENT: *LETHAL WEAPON*

It's three o'clock in the morning. You have to be up by seven to get to work on time. You just finished reading Chapter 11 of a great book. You hate to put it down. You flip through Chapter 12. It's only fourteen pages. Ten, twelve more minutes? What's another fifteen minutes—max—when the book has already guaranteed you're going to be sleepwalking in the morning. You read on. . . .

That's the kind of book you want to write, isn't it? The kind your reader can't put down? That's what we all want to write because we love gotta-keep-reading books so dearly. That's the kind of book that made most of us want to become writers. They are so compelling.

In case you don't already know, the best news I can share with you is that it isn't necessarily the most fantastic writing that keeps one reading. You don't have to write better than or even as well as _____ (fill in the blank with your all-time favorite author's name) to keep a reader reading way past his bedtime. Your writing can be genuinely mediocre. The *tension* you, the author, create in telling your story is what will compel a reader to keep reading and coming back for more of your stories.

There are lots of ways to create tension in a story. Shane Black, who wrote the screenplay for **Lethal Weapon**, used most of them.

The story begins as an unknown woman climbs onto a balcony rail and plunges to her death. Finding out she is a hooker reduces our surprise a bit. Boozy, doped-up, wrong-side-of-the-law characters die on a frequent basis in both the story world and the real world. The world they live in is much more dangerous than the world the rest of us occupy. We don't have any reason to feel threatened by her suicide. We have no reason to care other than the general isn't-that-sad reaction we have when any human dies.

QUICK TIP: 👉

"COMPELLING":

EDITOR'S DEFINITION: TO FORCE A READER TO KEEP READING.

AUTHOR'S DEFINITION: TO FORCE AN EDITOR TO KEEP READING.

Then we find out it wasn't just a suicide. She may have been induced to climb up on the rail and fall from the balcony. She would have died anyway from the poison someone gave her. That's a bit more of a threat. Murderers sometimes kill randomly. But we can still write it off because it isn't likely to happen to us. Unless we also live that kind of existence, we don't worry. She put herself in that scary world, in that situation that made her a much more likely victim. We don't have a stake in this character's death.

UPPING THE STAKES

Though we don't have any stake in this unknown hooker's death, Martin Riggs (Mel Gibson) and Roger Murtaugh (Danny Glover) do. It's their job to

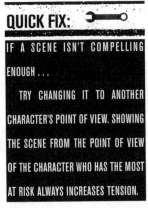

investigate the death and decide if it's something more than suicide. If there is a bad guy, they have to catch him, to stop him from murdering again.

Then we learn that, yes, there is a bad guy, probably more than one of them. Possibly a whole gang. More bad guys, more risk. The threat is suddenly a little bigger. Another woman dies, and the crime involves drugs. The bad guys (and the good guys) have more to lose or gain.

The cops discover that at least one of the criminals had been part of specially-trained Special Forces in Vietnam, like Riggs. That not only shows us a highly skilled and dangerous side of Riggs that we haven't seen thus far, but it also makes his opponents more formidable, skilled, and more dangerous, too.

Riggs and Murtaugh also discover that there is a huge shipment of drugs coming in. Besides upping the stakes again, this new knowledge sets a time bomb ticking.

A TIME BOMB

A time bomb—some writers call it a Ticking Clock or a Ticking Bomb—is one of the easier techniques to understand, and one any author can use to add page-turning suspense to her story. A time bomb is a goal with a deadline, and it's guaranteed to raise tension.

A time bomb sets a deadline for your protagonist or antagonist to do whatever it is she needs to do in order to reach an external or internal goal.

It automatically puts the pressure on. Your character not only has to do accomplish her goal—and it can be either a long-term goal or a short-term one—but she also has to do it in a prescribed period of time. The question becomes not only can your character do it, but can she do it in time.

For Riggs and Murtaugh, the question becomes, can they stop the bad guys before this big shipment of drugs comes in and floods the city they are supposed to protect with even more drugs.

Though *Lethal Weapon* isn't the best example of the use of time bombs, it does have several throughout. Murtaugh's realization toward the end of the movie provides another, "They know my address. They know where I live." Can Riggs and Murtaugh get to there before the bad guys do? If you were reading the story, you'd definitely turn to the next page.

CONFLICT BETWEEN CHARACTERS

The movie creates tension between the two main characters even before they meet. Riggs doesn't care about living and even has a death wish. Murtaugh has everything to live for. Because they have two such polar, opposite-ends-of-the-spectrum attitudes toward their lives, we see trouble ahead for this duo. That trouble is conflict, and conflict creates tension—but that is a whole other element you want in your fiction. It deserves its own chapter.

Lethal Weapon intertwines ever-increasing stakes, time bombs, and conflict, with the absolutely best technique for creating edge-of-your-seat suspense. The movie takes us up close and very personal.

GETTING PERSONAL

When things get personal the stakes really go up.

The unknown hooker turns out to be the daughter of an old friend of Murtaugh's. The case takes on a personal aspect because Murtaugh cares about someone who's affected. The father and Murtaugh served together in Vietnam, where the friend saved Murtaugh's life. Roger has more at stake now than solving a routine crime. Murtaugh's personal integrity and honor come into it now. Murtaugh owes him.

Riggs and Murtaugh go to talk to witnesses. At the first house, they are shot at and end up killing the guy they've gone to interview. As they approach the second house, it blows up. Had they been a few steps closer they could have been blown up, too. Investigating this crime is obviously hazardous to their health. That's personal.

Someone involved with the current badness/criminal activity was in the same Special Forces, a unit that represents a time Riggs looks back on with pride. Riggs takes that personally. His job is his life. He takes pride in his service and in the special skills he learned through his military experiences. Now *his* personal integrity and honor are involved. And someone tries to kill Riggs to get him out of the picture. This is a direct attack.

Someone kills Roger's daughter's boyfriend.

Someone has kidnapped Roger's daughter.

Eventually, the bad guys have Roger and Riggs, too.

What started as a random hooker's suicide has become a life-or-death struggle for our heroes. The stakes have gone up, and along the way it's become more and more personal. What's at stake by the end of the story is Riggs' and Murtaugh's very lives. And what's more personal than that?

BUT I'M NOT WRITING ACTION/ADVENTURE/SUSPENSE

By now there are a few of you on the edges of your seats, waiting in suspense to understand how all this applies to what you are writing. What if you want to write a relationship comedy or women's fiction or a historical saga? Upping the stakes, time bombs, and all of that other stuff are built in to a story like *Lethal Weapon*. In action/adventure/suspense genres those are an integral part. How does this apply to something like *Bridget Jones's Diary*?

Bridget sets a time bomb of sorts herself when she starts a diary and gives herself a year to reach her goal of not being alone. We don't really feel the clock ticking until we find that Darcy is leaving the country.

Though Bridget's relationships never reach the life-and-death proportions of *Lethal Weapon*, the stakes go up considerably all along the way. The stakes are emotional. Which of you didn't groan inside for Bridget when she asked Daniel, the scoundrel, if he loved her? We realized—even though she didn't—that she was putting more on the line than she should. And how high were the stakes when, after the fight between Mark and Daniel, she sends them *both* away? The countdown for her to reach her goal was slowly ticking away, and yet she upped the stakes.

In *While You Were Sleeping*, the stakes are high. Grandma—a woman Lucy doesn't even know—might have a heart attack if Lucy tells the truth and clears up the misunderstanding. Then she'll lose a whole family, one she desperately longs to be a part of. In the climax, Lucy realizes she can marry the wrong man and at least be part of that family, or she can tell the truth and lose everything: the man she's come to love and the family. That's also very personal.

There are several ticking clocks in the story. The biggest one Lucy starts herself is when she accepts Peter's proposal. Will something happen before Lucy's marriage to the wrong man? It's a problem with a deadline.

In *About a Boy*, Will (Hugh Grant) pretends he has a kid so that he can meet young single mothers. He's figured out that they are the perfect relationship material for a guy like himself—he considers them desperate and yet unwilling to commit. Then Marcus (Nicholas Hoult), the child of one young woman in the single-parent support group Will has been sneaking into, begins showing up on his doorstep because the boy needs a larger support system than just his mother. Marcus threatens the independent, I-don't-need-anyone persona that Will has carefully crafted. Those are characters with a huge conflict of interests, and it gets more and more personal as the story goes on. The stakes go up, and a time bomb starts ticking down to the boy committing "social suicide" by performing in a talent show at school to please his mother. Will has to save Marcus before the time bomb goes off.

In *Life As A House*, George Monroe (Kevin Kline) has a limited amount of time to straighten out his totally screwed up son, Sam (Hayden Christensen) and get close to him again. One can't find anything more personal or a louder ticking time bomb than a character who knows he is dying.

Speed is as perfect an example as you will find for adding tension to your story by using time bombs. The story has a definite time limit—the money must be delivered by a certain time—and the speed must be maintained at 50 mph. If either challenge is not met, the real bomb will go off.

Though controlling the speed is not a bomb based on time, the effects are the same. Any goal with very specific limits attached adds suspense to a story. Even without a clock ticking, the technique ratchets up tension.

We see time bombs used, short- and medium-term, to set limits all through *Speed*. At the beginning, the elevator is going to fall. The action makes that clear. If Harry and Jack don't get the people out in time, they will fall with it. The detonator ticks more loudly with each creak and slip of the elevator. Even the creaks and slips are tiny ticking time bombs. If the elevator slips while they are getting someone out, that person could be cut in half or decapitated. The viewer breathes easier after each passenger is off and feels the tension start to rise again as attention is turned to the next passenger.

There are medium-term time limits that last for several scenes. If Jack doesn't catch the bus, the driver may let the speed fall because he doesn't know there is a problem. If they don't get the bus refueled quickly enough, the bus will stop. All of those limits play into the long-term, overall time bomb that will explode if the speed and time limits aren't met.

But why do we care? What the heck does this have to do with you? With your life? What gets you emotionally involved while you're watching *Speed*? Why should you care what happens to Riggs or Murtaugh or his daughter or anyone else while you're watching *Lethal Weapon*?

They're movies. Made-up stories. How did the writers make you care?

The storyteller and his characters—Riggs and Murtaugh in the case of *Lethal Weapon*—all speak the universal language.

THE UNIVERSAL LANGUAGE = READER IDENTIFICATION

The universal language is emotion. The writer gets to us with emotion. He shows us how the characters feel. When he gives us reason to empathize or sympathize, we feel the emotion, too. We're hooked. We care.

The first time we meet him, Riggs makes us laugh—makes us feel emotion. We think he's a bit nuts, but we like him. His funny Three Stooges imitation amuses us, but why is he risking his life? Then we find out he's suicidal. His wife has died. He has nothing to live for and cares about living even less. We quickly understand why he amuses himself by taking chances that we consider outrageous.

We also get a hint of his humanity when a sniper draws his ire after shooting a child. He doesn't care much about his own life, but he values the life of an innocent child. The only thing that keeps him from swallowing the special bullet he keeps for just such a purpose is "the job." Doing the job gives him a reason to live. But his attitude encourages him to take risks he probably wouldn't take if he wasn't, as the police psychiatrist describes him, "suicidal, perhaps psychotic."

Most of us can understand—and identify with—grief. The very few who haven't felt it, have felt the dread of the inevitability of it, if they've ever loved anyone at all. We like Riggs. We sympathize with him. We identify with him. We feel for and with him.

QUICK FIX:

IF YOUR STORY DOESN'T HAVE ENOUGH EMOTION . . .

PLAY THE *WHY* GAME. WHY DOES THIS CHARACTER FEEL THIS WAY? WHY IS HE AFRAID (INDIFFERENT, EXCITED, FOOLHARDY, ETC.)? WHY DOES HE WANT X? HAVE YOU PUT ENOUGH DETAILS EXPLAINING THE *WHY* ON THE PAGE TO MAKE THE REASON(S) CLEAR TO THE READER? CLARITY WILL OFTEN TRANSLATE TO A STRONGER EMOTIONAL CONNECTION WITH THE READER.

Murtaugh is Rigg's opposite. He has everything to live for. He worries that he's getting too old for his job and that something will happen to him before he can retire and enjoy the wonderful life he has made for himself. He has a wonderful family, a house, a cat. He's just turned 50. Upon our introduction to Roger Murtaugh, we feel warmth. We see a family celebrating a man's birthday with a humor and intimacy that shows us how close and loving this family is. Anyone who has lived with a close and loving family probably feels sentimental. Anyone who hasn't experienced that kind of family life probably feels a wistful longing.

And anyone whose life is a mixture of good days and bad—and whose isn't?—has probably also experienced a form of Roger's things-are-going-too-well pessimism. If we've had too many good days or experiences in a row, most of us find ourselves waiting for something to ruin it all. Murtaugh's whole life is too good, and he's feeling like maybe he should quit his dangerous job before something or someone messes up that wonderful life.

When the two meet, Murtaugh fears, and rightly so, that Riggs, with his suicidal bent, is exactly the thing he's been worried about. Murtaugh immediately feels he and his dreams are at risk. Riggs might mess everything up. The audience joins in, suspecting the same thing, but hoping Murtaugh is wrong. We've grown to like and feel attached and sympathetic to Riggs. Now we simultaneously feel empathy and sympathy for Murtaugh, too. Instant tension.

And we *care* what happens to both of them.

By giving us characters we understand because we universally feel their same emotions, the writer has put the audience in a position where he can manipulate our feelings. We're involved now. We care what happens next.

Making a reader care—and feel that emotion—is perhaps the trickiest thing a writer must do. Emotional intensity makes a book worth buying—and reading. You achieve that through your characters' emotions.

Every emotion is universal. Love. Hate. Jealousy. Happiness. Fear. No matter what verbal language passes our lips, emotion is the one language that we all speak and understand.

Let's take one emotion—love—and look at one extremely universal type of it. Let's look at the maternal kind. Everyone—no matter where you grew up or what language you speak or what color your skin or what you believe—everyone can understand what it means to have a mother's love. Either they have felt it, or they have felt the lack of it and experienced the detrimental effects of wanting it. It's basic. It's universal.

Think for a moment about your favorite stories, whether books or movies. How many protagonists can you think of who seem to have no mother? Either she's deceased or distant—or not even mentioned. Or, if a major character does have a mother, it's rare that she is "normal." The relationship between her and the main charecter is often unhealthy in some way. (The mother is overbearing or obnoxious or dependent or uncaring or domineering or . . . whatever.) Have you ever wondered why?

Now think of the bad guys. Many of them have mothers still in the picture. And those mothers are almost universally as crazy as loons. Again, why?

I'm sure you see the answer for yourself. We are supposed to identify and buy in to the character's emotions. A mother's relationship with her child is one sure way—a guarantee, if you will—that we all will see what influenced him and made him who he is. Therefore, we'll understand and identify with at least one aspect of a character.

Though most writers don't consciously set out to create pitiful, mother-less characters, we do have to explain what made our characters who they are. Nothing explains and motivates certain characteristics better than that character's mother—or lack of one.

Besides motivation and reader identification, there are other reasons why writers don't give characters a huge personal support system of family and friends. The best reason is so the character has only himself to rely on to get out of the messes the writer has put him in. When it all comes down to one person—think *Jaws*—and that one person has no one and nothing else to rely on, that also creates tension.

QUICK FIX: ⌐━━○

IF SOMETHING IN YOUR STORY STRETCHES CREDIBILITY . . .

MOTIVATE, MOTIVATE, MOTIVATE. LOOK AT THE *WHY* SOMEONE IS DOING THE LESS-THAN-CREDIBLE THING OR THE *REASON* SOME STRANGE THING IS HAPPENING. KEEP DIGGING FOR REASONS UNTIL YOU FIND ONE THAT IS UNDERSTANDABLE AND BELIEVABLE. IF YOU CAN'T FIND A LOGICAL REASON, YOU'LL HAVE TO WORK BACKWARD TO ADD IT, OR THE SOMETHING WILL HAVE TO GO.

INCITING EMOTION

Though every emotion is universal, what incites an emotion is not. Fear is a prime example.

If I see a mouse in my kitchen, quicker than you can say boo, I will have a string of chairs lined up across the room to walk on until the mouse is caught. I don't harbor an illogical fear. I have my reasons. When I was a kid—age four, maybe five—one of my friends was rushed to the hospital in the middle of the night because a mouse had bitten her. It somehow got into her bed and tangled in her sheets, and she was bitten many times as it tried to escape. I don't remember her name. I barely remember the friend at all . . . . I do remember the mouse. I do remember my parents discussing it at the breakfast table the next morning. I remember feeling terrified.

If I wrote a story with a mouse and had the main character walking around her kitchen on chairs you might think she was irrational—unless you also knew her past experiences. I'd probably use ones such as I described when I told you about my fear of mice. In the story, my character would have been the little girl rushed to the hospital in the middle of the night, bitten from head to toe by a mouse trapped in the sheets. She'd still have scars. You'd then find her fear logical.

Logic is the only thing that creates believable motivation. Understandable motivation creates sympathetic emotion. That doesan't mean the reader would start walking around the kitchen on chairs. It does mean the reader would understand *why* the charecter does it. Understanding a character's motivation doesn't necessarily mean you also share her fears.

By giving your characters past experiences that tweak logical emotions in the present, you create sympathetic emotion. The reader subconsciously thinks, "If *I* were in that same situation, with the same exact background, having the experiences this character is going through, I'd feel/react exactly the same way."

Instant sympathy. Instant reader identification. That's what you want.

QUICK TIP: 👉

IF YOU WANT YOUR READER TO CRY . . . MAKE YOUR CHARACTER HOLD BACK HER TEARS. IF THE CHARACTER CRIES, YOUR READER DOESN'T HAVE TO. THIS APPLIES TO ALL EMOTIONS. IF YOUR CHARACTER *RELEASES* OR *EXPRESSES* THE EMOTION—STRIKES OUT IN RAGE, JUMPS UP AND DOWN FOR JOY, ETC.—IT TAKES THE PRESSURE OFF THE READER TO FEEL THE EMOTION.

Think of a so-so book you've read recently. You may not even remember the title or the main character's name. It was an okay story but . . . .

Another person, somewhere, may very well have thought the same story was wonderful. She may have laughed out loud or shed a tear or two. She might even think it was the best book she'd read in several years. Why? What makes a difference?

Why does one person read the whole night through while another person reading the same book reads it in fits and starts, maybe taking a week or two to finish? It depends a lot on personal experience.

Say the book is set on a ranch. You've never visited one or wanted to. Say the protagonist grew up in a family of eight, and you were an only child. Perhaps her goal is to escape her little hometown and travel the world. You've been most of the places you want to go and find you like home better than any of them. Your life experiences, your wants and dreams color how you react to a particular character's story.

The key here is obvious: If you can make your reader identify—that's where logic comes in—with what your characters are feeling, your reader will understand the characters and feel for them. The more a reader identifies with the emotions, the more he will feel them for your characters, and the more wrapped up that reader will be in your story.

So if you want to find the widest audience possible for your work, you have to give your characters dreams and goals and experiences that the majority of readers can logically identify with, understand, and, therefore, feel. Your characters have to act on those emotions in ways most people can understand.

Though most of us do not have the resources or training to go after someone who kidnapped our child, we understand why Murtaugh uses everything at his command to do so. Like him, we would use every resource we had to do whatever we needed to do in order to rescue our own child. Based on our own emotions, if we fully understand why these characters act and react the way they do, we go along breathlessly for the exciting ride.

Your readers have their own hopes and fears and emotions—and reasons for them. If a reader understands your characters' reasons for feeling the way they do, if they can feel that if they were in the same situation, with the same skills, resources, background, and baggage, they would react and feel exactly the same way your characters do, you have established Reader Identification.

We've all felt every feeling Riggs and Murtaugh experienced throughout the movie. Maybe not to the same degree and probably not for the same reasons, but emotions feel the same no matter why you feel them. If you twist those emotions by getting more and more personal, your reader will turn the page. Up the reader's tension again by upping whatever your character has at stake. Start a time bomb ticking, and you'll notch those emotions up again. Your character's feelings will become even more intense.

The reader will feel the character's emotions . . . and be up reading until three o'clock in the morning.

Chapter Seven

Conflict

ASSIGNMENT: *THE SIXTH SENSE*

Look in any dictionary for the definition of "conflict," and you'll find the following meanings: fight, disagreement, opposition; an emotional disturbance, a prolonged physical struggle, a clash, an inability to reconcile, a struggle with realistic or moral considerations.

That definition gives you a wide variety of the types of conflicts you can use in telling your characters' stories, but one word–*struggle*–tells you everything you need to know about conflict. Struggle should be a key component of every element in your story, whether the struggle is mental, physical, or emotional; whether the struggle is with himself or with other characters; whether the struggle is to overcome an obstacle that is solid– such as a brick wall blocking his path–or imaginary–something all in the character's mind.

Go back to the beginning of the book (except the introduction) and skim your way through the various examples. You will find something in each chapter—whether it is specifically called conflict or not—that qualifies as a struggle.

In the chapter on Characterization (*While You Were Sleeping*), Jack has character traits that cause a clash between the attraction he feels for Lucy and the moral considerations he feels toward his brother and his family.

In *Spider-man*, Peter struggles with a variety of obstacles in his efforts to reach his goal. The struggle with the Green Goblin is not the best example, but it is a perfect example of a prolonged physical conflict. The Goblin keeps coming back, scene after scene after scene.

When characters are built to prove or disprove a premise, an ongoing struggle is automatic as your character travels from point A to point B, from direction-challenged to having direction, as Cher does in *Clueless*. Cher struggles to keep believing she is right when everything that happens should tell her she is wrong. Once she comes to her senses, she struggles to make things right.

In the chapter on Internal Goals, Jack (*Speed*) has sharp opposition (a struggle) with the bad guy, but an even sharper opposition (struggle) with himself until he learns to believe he can win using his brains.

Riggs and Murtaugh have opposing attitudes toward life in *Lethal Weapon*: one loves it; the other could care less if it goes on. We know there will be tension—and a struggle

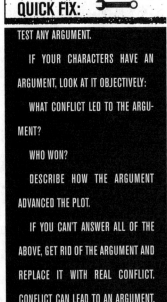

QUICK FIX:

TEST ANY ARGUMENT.

IF YOUR CHARACTERS HAVE AN ARGUMENT, LOOK AT IT OBJECTIVELY: WHAT CONFLICT LED TO THE ARGUMENT?

WHO WON?

DESCRIBE HOW THE ARGUMENT ADVANCED THE PLOT.

IF YOU CAN'T ANSWER ALL OF THE ABOVE, GET RID OF THE ARGUMENT AND REPLACE IT WITH REAL CONFLICT. CONFLICT CAN LEAD TO AN ARGUMENT, BUT AN ARGUMENT IS NOT CONFLICT.

between them—before they even meet.

You may not come up with the same examples I've listed because there are many to choose from. The point of this small exercise is to recognize conflict when you see it.

Conflict doesn't happen by accident.

From the moment characters start to take form in your mind, *your* struggle should be to build in the characteristics that put them in direct opposition with the other characters and with the premise you want to prove. Your struggle should be to give them goals that will force *them* to struggle to reach their goals. If you shape your characters that way, conflict will come as surely as winter comes in Antarctica, based solely on who your characters are. Best selling author Sandra Brown put it this way in a writing workshop I was fortunate enough to attend: "If your hero is a fireman, your heroine had better be an arsonist." In his book, *Fiction is Folks*, Robert Newton Peck describes conflict even more simply: Two dogs. One bone.

In creating conflict, you have to consider the kind of obstacles you will present for your protagonist to overcome. The obstacles must present appropriate challenges for your character. An eight-year-old kid stealing a lollipop wouldn't present much of a challenge to Spider-man, but dealing with that same child would present a huge challenge to a brand-new step-father, if it was his stepson and he was trying to develop a solid relationship with him.

QUICK TIP:

CONFLICT IS ABOUT COURAGE.

FOR EVERY ELEMENT OF CONFLICT IN THE STORY YOU ARE TELLING, ASK: DOES FACING THIS OBSTACLE REQUIRE COURAGE ON THE PART OF THIS CHARACTER? IF THE OBSTACLE DOES NOT TAKE COURAGE FOR THIS PARTICULAR CHARACTER, IT IS NOT APPROPRIATE AND WILL WEAKEN YOUR STORY.

It takes planning to incrementally change your hero into the person he needs to become to finally conquer his demons—whatever they are—and reach his goals. For example, if your protagonist needs to learn assertiveness, you can't have him buckling to every person he meets along the way, then suddenly show him sticking up for himself on the last page, merely because it is crucial for your story to have a satisfying ending.

It takes planning to keep your reader turning pages, wondering if your hero has the courage it will take for him to overcome the challenges you've made him face. If your hero keeps digging deeper, and finds more courage, and still deeper and finds a little more, your reader will feel a sense of inevitability as he turns the last page and finds that the hero manages to find a bit more for his final test. You want that reader doubting all along, and yet thinking at the end, "I should have seen that coming."

And wasn't that exactly how you felt the first time you saw *The Sixth Sense*? Every time I watch it, I am more and more amazed that I didn't see it coming. It was there in black and white and living color. In spades. But I guess that's enough clichés, and it's time to issue a warning: Anyone who hasn't seen the movie, do it now! Put down this book. Don't read this chapter until you've seen the movie. It's probably too late to keep secrets, with the length of time the movie has been out, but don't let me ruin the I-should-have-seen-it-coming for you. *The Sixth Sense* is an excellent movie for all the elements, characterization, goals, etc., we've discussed to this point, but the awe of discovery is invaluable to our dissection of conflict.

MALCOLM'S GOALS

Malcolm's (Bruce Willis) internal goal—the internal goal most of us at least subconsciously recognized—is clearly defined in the first few minutes of the movie. His wife reads the plaque he has just been presented, proudly articulating his "sacrifice and commitment" to the children of Philadelphia and says, "You have put everything second, including me." It doesn't sound like criticism since she lovingly adds, "You have a gift."

We immediately move to his external goal. He finds that a former patient, one he didn't help, has broken into his home. "What do you want?" Malcolm asks the gun-wielding young man.

"What you promised me," Vincent (Donnie Wahlberg) cries.

There are layers of conflict in the dialogue in this scene. "Don't you remember your own patients?" Vincent taunts. Malcolm has just been feeling pleased about the award he won. Should he be acclaimed when he can't even remember his patients?

Besides the conflict of the physical threat the former patient represents, logically, Malcolm must also be struggling to reconcile the award he just accepted with this realistic failure confronting him face-to-face.

"I waited ten years for you." How did an award-winning doctor let this troubled patient just disappear without knowing—or wanting to know—what happened to him? The young boy has obviously gone through a prolonged struggle. Wouldn't the sacrificing and committed man his wife has just described follow his patient closely enough to see what happened to him, especially since Malcolm obviously didn't cure him?

"I remember you as very compassionate." Malcolm finally remembers Vincent and struggles to use his gift. It doesn't work.

"You forgot cursed." Vincent hurls the accusation. "You failed me." He then shoots Malcolm and turns the gun on himself.

Six months later: Malcolm has obviously recovered and has returned to his work, trying to help children. By the circled items displayed on the notes he is reading, we know he has a new patient. One who shares the same profile—divorced parents, acute anxiety, socially isolated, possible mood disorder—as Vincent, his failure, had. Knowing all the mental and emotional turmoil Malcolm's failure has probably caused him, we understand that he will be especially determined not to fail this child. We see his external goal.

COLE'S CONFLICT WITH MALCOLM

Our first introduction to Cole (Haley Joel Osment) shows him hustling toward a church. We see his fright. When Malcolm follows Cole inside, we see that Cole is hanging out and quietly playing between the pews. The screenwriter, M. Night Shyamalan, shows us Cole's fear. We guess that he is seeking sanctuary even before Malcolm subtly tells Cole that he has caught on to the fact that Cole's goal is to find sanctuary from his fear.

Malcolm's job (and the key to reaching his external goal) will be to discover and help Cole deal with whatever he's afraid of, to cure him of his fear.

As Cole and Malcolm's first meeting ends, Cole asks, "Are you a good doctor?" Conflict for Cole: He struggles with hope. He wants Malcolm to be a good doctor. He wants someone to help him. Conflict for Malcolm: He failed a patient like Cole before. He wants to be able to say he is a good doctor. He wants to live up to the award he won. He can't. "I used to be," he says. "I won an award once." He struggles with the fact that he can't forthrightly answer "Yes."

Shortly thereafter, at their second meeting, Cole tells Malcolm, "You're nice, but you can't help me." This key line of dialogue throws up another obstacle. Malcolm is going to have a real struggle on his hands if he is going to reach his external goal. How can Malcolm help Cole—making up for his failure with Vincent—if Cole doesn't plan to see or cooperate with him?

The next time they meet, Malcolm is walking with Cole to school. We logically assume that Malcolm is trying to overcome Cole's reluctance to work with him by just showing up where Cole is likely to be. Cole admits that he doesn't want his mother thinking he is a freak. She's obviously the only one he can count on to not think of him that way yet, and he has carefully constructed his world to keep her from knowing.

When Malcolm tells Cole definitively that he, Malcolm, doesn't think Cole is a freak either, we suspect Malcolm has advanced his cause. Cole may not be willing to trust Malcolm completely yet, but Cole will put up with Malcolm to have another human being around who doesn't think he is a freak.

And finally, mid-point through the movie, we get to the crux of the matter.

AND THE CONFLICT *REALLY* GETS INTENSE

Cole asks Malcolm to tell him a story about why he is sad.

At first Malcolm says he isn't supposed to talk about "stuff like that." But Cole withdraws again and turns away. Malcolm quietly begins to tell of his failure with Vincent, and how all of that has changed his relationship with his wife.

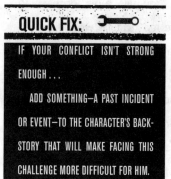

QUICK FIX:

IF YOUR CONFLICT ISN'T STRONG ENOUGH . . .

ADD SOMETHING—A PAST INCIDENT OR EVENT—TO THE CHARACTER'S BACK-STORY THAT WILL MAKE FACING THIS CHALLENGE MORE DIFFICULT FOR HIM.

Telling the story has helped. Cole has turned back to face Malcolm again. He's receptive. (Body language in this whole scene is very telling.)

"And then one day," Malcolm continues the story, "Malcolm meets this wonderful little boy." Malcolm explains that this very cool little boy reminds him of the other one, and Malcolm believes that if he can help this new boy, it will be like helping that other one.

"How's the story end?" Cole asks.

When Malcolm admits he doesn't know, Cole sighs and closes his eyes. We can almost see him considering. After another deep sigh, he says, "I want to tell you my secret now."

The viewer knows that Malcolm has gained Cole's trust. Malcolm has overcome another obstacle. But in the very next line of dialogue, we learn the secret and know that gaining Cole's trust was minor compared with the new and ten times more daunting obstacle.

Malcolm verifies just how far out of reach he fears his goal is when he records his thoughts later. Using words like paranoid and hallucinating, he says, "(Cole's) pathology is more severe than originally accessed." He adds grimly, "I'm not helping him."

So even *after* we know the secret, we do not see the facts. Like Malcolm, we're too busy bracing ourselves for the struggle Anna, his wife, articulated so well in the very first scene when she said, "You have a gift for teaching children how to be strong in situations where most adults would piss on themselves." That is exactly what we see. We see *conflict* ahead. And we can't or don't see the forest for the trees.

Because of the obvious goal and the rock solid motivation Mr. Shyamalan has established for Malcolm, we are focused on the conflict (the trees) Malcolm faces now. And that is how Shyamalan kept his secret (the forest) from the vast majority of us throughout the whole movie. He used what is known in storytelling as a McGuffin.

THE MCGUFFIN

Don't confuse a McGuffin with the famous red herring that mystery writers use to great effect when they are giving the reader lots of options about "who done it." A red herring is a choice. A McGuffin is a distraction more like the sleight of hand a magician would use to surprise you when he pulls a rabbit from a hat.

McGuffin is the word Alfred Hitchcock used to describe his most famous plot device. It helped seal his reputation as the cinematic "King of Suspense." A McGuffin is something, a plot device or element, that attracts the audience's attention and drives the plot forward.

Hitchcock used McGuffins in many of his films. The McGuffin in *North by Northwest* was the very vague "government secrets" his characters were chasing. Hitchcock, himself, described the government secrets as his "emptiest, most non-existent McGuffin." They were not important. We never even found out what the government secrets were. What was important was that his characters believed in them—the something that was nothing—and carried us right along with them.

Hitchcock perfected the plot device in his 1960 movie, *Psycho*. The whole first half of the movie was about a robbery, Janet Leigh's part in it, and her flight. But is a robbery how or what you remember about the movie? Hitchcock's McGuffin in that movie was stolen money—$40,000—but the only thing it really had to do with the main story he was telling—the story of a psycho killer—was that it got Janet Leigh to the Bates Motel.

Most explanations of Hitchcock's McGuffin describe it as something concrete—stolen money, government secrets, etc.—that turns out to be nothing of significance. The essential part of a McGuffin—and I think the part that helped seal Hitchcock's fame—is not the *something* that turns out to be nothing consequential. The important thing about a McGuffin is that it attracts the attention of the audience (and moves the plot forward) while distracting them from focusing on something else.

Shyamalan twisted Hitchcock's classic McGuffin. Instead of using "something," he used conflict, an essential story element, to distract our attention from the facts he laid out for all the world to see. Malcolm's external goal—to help Cole—and the conflict it presented—how will Malcolm ever overcome that huge obstacle?—distracted us from the obvious. We anticipated the struggle, the conflict, and totally missed the fact that became so clear at the end of the movie: We missed the fact that Malcolm was dead.

Using plot elements like goals and conflict to distract the audience is the ultimate McGuffin. Malcolm's overt goal—to help Cole—turns into nothingness once we see the whole picture. From Cole's perspective, Malcolm is just another ghost, come to haunt and torture him. And we find that Malcolm's real goal—whether he set it for himself or not—is to come to terms and accept his own death.

Once Cole reveals his secret—he can see dead people—to Malcolm, the viewer thinks Malcolm's next obstacle is to believe the unbelievable for Cole's sake. We discover instead, that Malcolm has to believe the unbelievable so that he can do what he needs to do and go on. We think his final obstacle is finding a solution to Cole's problem. In a stunning twist, we discover that Cole has to help Malcolm discover the solution to his own problem.

COLE'S *REAL* GOALS AND CONFLICTS

Cole is a terrified little boy. His internal goal is to quit being afraid. When Malcolm asks Cole to think of something he wants from their sessions, Cole asks, "Can it be something I don't want?" Then clarifies. "I don't want to be scared anymore."

Cole is sitting in the kitchen when we are introduced to his mother (Toni Collette). She walks in and sees the cabinets she just closed, all hanging open again.

"What are you thinking?" he asks. "Anything bad about me?"

We've seen the scratches on his arms. Up until now, we've worried that she may have caused them. We see her response and interaction with him. Though we don't understand exactly what's wrong, we're relieved to recognize that it probably isn't child abuse. She's deeply concerned about her child, and when the tension we thought we saw in him is verified by the sweaty palm print he leaves behind on the table when he goes to school, we sigh with relief that we aren't going to have to watch this child we've come to care about be abused. We're very relieved at her sincere concern.

And we understand his question about whether she was thinking anything bad about him when, once they are out of sight of his mother, his friend hands Cole the backpack he offered to carry and calls him a freak. It's so important to Cole that his mother doesn't think of him that way, that he goes to great lengths (his struggle) to ensure that she keeps thinking of him as a normal kid. He pays another kid to act like his friend, solely for her benefit. And that effort on her behalf means he has to put up with more, not fewer, instances where he must be mocked and called names. That obstacle—putting up with the name-calling and cruelty—is incredibly difficult for him, we realize, once we understand his external goal.

Cole dearly wants to be normal. He wants to be the first kid selected when his schoolmates are choosing sports teams. He wants people not to look at him "like that." To reach his external goal and be normal, he must reach his internal goal. Though at this point we haven't seen the reason (the why), we do understand that Cole's internal goal is in serious conflict with his external goal. No one will ever think he is normal as long as he runs around acting like a terrified weirdo. He has a real struggle on his hands.

Cole's goals seem to be a perfect match with Malcolm's. Cole's goal is to be normal. That, on the surface, is exactly in line with what Malcolm wants. By dealing with all those things we saw circled on that scribbled page of notes—Cole's parent's divorce, his social isolation, his possible mood disorders, and his acute anxiety—we expect Malcolm to help Cole become normal.

Cole's internal goal also seems to coincide with Malcolm's. Cole wants to stop being afraid. Still well and good. It's on Malcolm's list of things to deal with: acute anxiety.

Trust is something Cole is reluctant to give. He struggles with it. Somewhere along the way, he's figured out that seeing dead people is not normal. A large part of his challenge up until now has been trying to seem normal when he knows he's not. He has learned to draw pictures of rainbows instead of dead men with screwdrivers jabbed into their necks. He's learned to pay Tommy Tomasino to fool his mother into believing he is normal enough to have friends. Not only is he scared by the ghosts he sees, he is terrified of people finding out his secret.

In Malcolm, Cole has finally found someone he can reveal his secret to and not fear being called a freak. Getting Malcolm to believe him will be his next struggle. At least that's what we think. We don't see and don't understand exactly how intense Cole's conflict is, unless you're one of the rare ones who got it right away.

CONFLICT TO DIE FOR

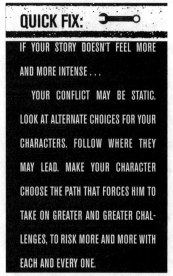

QUICK FIX:

IF YOUR STORY DOESN'T FEEL MORE AND MORE INTENSE . . .

YOUR CONFLICT MAY BE STATIC. LOOK AT ALTERNATE CHOICES FOR YOUR CHARACTERS. FOLLOW WHERE THEY MAY LEAD. MAKE YOUR CHARACTER CHOOSE THE PATH THAT FORCES HIM TO TAKE ON GREATER AND GREATER CHALLENGES, TO RISK MORE AND MORE WITH EACH AND EVERY ONE.

Most of us watched Cole struggle to decide whether or not to trust Malcolm with his secret without all the information we needed to understand how really gargantuan his conflict was at this point. Knowing what we know now, let's look at the crucial and revealing conversation between Cole and Malcolm.

After Malcolm finishes his sad story about his relationship with his wife, we see Cole's internal struggle through body language. He sighs deeply. He closes his eyes. He takes a deep breath and sighs again—and, finally, Cole quietly says "I want to tell you my secret now."

We can break this down line by line to see how carefully it is constructed.

Cole: "I see dead people." (He sighs deeply and watches Malcolm very closely.)

Malcolm: "In your dreams?" (Malcolm struggles not to react with dismay. And this line is part of the McGuffin. We're still concentrating on how and whether Malcolm will be able to reach this child and help him. Whammy! The revelation is a *huge* obstacle to that goal!)

When Cole indicates "no" with a shake of his head, Malcolm goes on.

"While you're awake?" (He's still trying to grasp the enormity of the obstacle.)

Cole slowly nods "Yes."

Malcolm: (carefully controlling his expression) "Dead people like in graves? In coffins?"

Cole: (Shakes head again and hesitantly, watching very closely—his eyes never leave Malcolm as he says) "Walking around like regular people." (Pause. Malcolm is dead. Malcolm walks around like regular people. Will Malcolm *get* it? If Malcolm gets it, will he get mad and hurt him like others have? When Malcolm doesn't react, Cole continues.) "They don't see each other. They only see what they want to see." (Again, he studies Malcolm for his reaction and takes another really deep breath. If Malcolm—the only hope Cole finally dares to feel—gets it, Malcolm may go away. If Malcolm goes away, Cole loses his last hope that someone can help him.)

The first time we watch this movie, we don't see the extreme force of conflict between their two goals since they seem so closely aligned. But Malcolm can't reach his goal of helping Cole if Cole won't see or talk to him. Cole can't reach his goal of not seeing dead people if he sees Malcolm—since Malcolm is dead.

By telling Malcolm his secret, Cole risks everything. He can tell and risk losing the person who might be able to help him. Or he can not tell and lose any hope of getting the help he so desperately needs.

They both face a struggle, a seemingly insurmountable obstacle. That is conflict.

Real, solid conflict puts your characters in a place where they are forced—at least once in your story—to choose between two different ways of risking everything they want.

Look at the movies previously discussed. In *While You Were Sleeping*, Lucy has to choose between not saying anything and getting the family she wants, but forever losing the man she loves, or telling the truth and possibly losing the family *and* the man she loves.

In *Speed* when the bus is running out of fuel, Jack has to choose between trying to get everyone off—and possibly getting everyone blown up—or waiting for a better solution,all the while knowing that everyone will blow up if the bus runs out of fuel and slows to below 50 mph.

Now you can consider the rest of the movies, remembering that, because you know the story, you know the heroes made the right choices. When you watched the very first time, you didn't have any idea how it would all play out. You had no idea if the choices the heroes made were good or disastrous. When you're planning your story, play with where alternate choices will take you. Know what the characters' options are.

There are several other things you should consider when developing the obstacles that will create the conflict for your characters. The conflict can neither stay static nor go from teeny, tiny challenges straight to huge obstacles, without risking losing your reader. If you've heard of rising conflict, you know that each obstacle has to be a bit more challenging than the one before.

In *Speed*, the obstacles Jack faced were not limited to keeping the speed at 50. That was only the initial challenge. First, it was keeping the speed up when the bus driver didn't know he *needed* to do so, then it was keeping the speed up in traffic; then it was keeping the speed up in traffic when there wasn't a driver because he'd been injured. Then it was keeping the speed up in traffic and approaching a stoplight that turned red. Then it was keeping the speed up while turning a corner. When they took care of the traffic problem by getting off the freeway and onto a road that was under construction, they faced the challenge of jumping a large gap in the highway. If speed had been and remained the only problem, the conflict would have been static. And we would have been very bored. As it was, the problems became more devastating, and we inched closer to the edges of our seats with each one.

> **QUICK TIP:**
>
> MAKE A LIST.
>
> MAKE A LIST OF EACH OBSTACLE YOU PLAN FOR YOUR CHARACTER TO FACE. IMAGINE YOU HAVE A COURAGE METER AND EVALUATE WHETHER THE NEEDLE RISES CONTINUALLY WITH EACH ONE. ARRANGE AND REARRANGE THE OBSTACLES UNTIL YOU HAVE THEM IN AN ORDER THAT WILL FORCE THE CHARACTER TO GAIN MORE COURAGE AND GROW WITH EACH ONE.

If the challenges had jumped from maintaining speed to jumping the gap in the highway, and then back to getting through a busy intersection after the light turned red, we would have felt bewildered and like we had whiplash. The movie wouldn't have gotten the word-of-mouth excitement that kept the theaters packed. Characters have to struggle with incremental challenges to get strong enough to face the next one. Conflict works hand in hand with character growth.

When Jack first discovered the problem with the bus, he didn't immediately risk getting the passengers off. He negotiated for the release of one—and learned the bad guy was serious about blowing up the bus because he blew up a second passenger who tried to get off when they transferred the injured man. Jack then relied on his partner and others to rescue them. He tried to disable the bomb. Each struggle was a little bit tougher. And Jack grew into facing the final challenge—and believing that he could win.

Cole didn't instantly grow into trusting Malcolm to help him in *The Sixth Sense*. He had to see that Malcolm wasn't going to hurt him. He had to learn that Malcolm would keep coming back, even after Cole had turned him away. He had to see that Malcolm didn't consider Cole a freak, even after he revealed that he paid someone to pretend to be his friend.

Once Cole reaches the point where he has grown to trust Malcolm enough to reveal his biggest secret, he struggles to make Malcolm believe and help him—even though he also knows that if Malcolm believes the secret, he will eventually have to face the fact that he is dead.

And that is the heart of the final conflict—the one we didn't see.

THE ULTIMATE STRUGGLE

Cole's next struggle is to convince Malcolm he's telling the truth. He's not just hallucinating or lying about things like bumblebee pins—as his mother suspects. Though the audience now sees the ghosts Cole sees—and is rooting for Malcolm to believe and help him—Malcolm asks, "Are you sure they're there?"

Both of them are frustrated. Malcolm thinks he's going to fail this patient, too. He gives up. "I can't be your doctor anymore," he tells Cole.

"Don't fail me," Cole cries. "Don't give up. You're the only one who can help me. I know it."

By the time Malcolm believes, Cole has gone back to being sarcastic and distant . . . and to finding sanctuary at the church. Malcolm finds him there and asks Cole what the ghosts want.

Cole's experiences with Malcolm give him an answer he hadn't considered before now. He's learned from Malcolm that the man is there because he wants *help*. He wants to resolve the things he didn't before he died. When he tells Malcolm he thinks the ghosts want help, the conflict resolutions begin to fall into place.

Cole helps the ghost of the little girl show her father that the young sister might be at risk from the deadly mother too. He hasn't stopped seeing ghosts, but he has stopped being so afraid of them. He now knows what to do when he sees dead people.

He's starting to act—and fit in—more normally with the other kids. He gets a part he wants in the school play. He's smiling and playfully happy as he bids Malcolm good-bye. Cole suggests that Malcolm might try talking to his wife—when she's asleep.

Malcolm has helped him. We think they've both reached their external goals. The story gives us an extra bit of assurance that Cole is going to be all right—he's going to be able to achieve some sense of normalcy—when he tells his mother he is ready to communicate. We know he is in good hands. She will be there with help when he needs it. Though it isn't really Cole's conflict resolution—technically, that's already done—it is a nice confirmation after the emotional roller coaster we've been on with him, and it does help resolve his mother's conflict; she wants them to be a family that's doing more than just surviving.

Then Malcolm goes home to reach his internal goal. And we discover that Malcolm is resolving his external goal, too. He realizes—at about the same time we do—that he is dead. He accepts it and tells Anna that she was never second-place. His conflict is over. He's reached both of his goals. Now he can go.

ORDERLY RESOLUTIONS

There is one last thing about the conflict in this story that is worth noting. Both Malcolm and Cole's conflicts were resolved in the reverse order that they were introduced. We found out Cole's goals—both internal and external—after we understood Malcolm's. But Cole's conflicts were resolved before we got to Malcolm's. Malcolm's internal goal was established in the first few minutes of the movie when his wife said he put everything second, including her. But it was the very last conflict resolved in the story. Though a perfectly reversed order isn't mandatory in every story—whether novel or movie—it seems to work that way in the most satisfying ones.

QUICK TIP:

BE MEAN.

IF YOU WANT TO CREATE GREAT CONFLICT, ASK YOURSELF EVERY TIME YOU SIT DOWN AT YOUR TYPEWRITER, "HOW CAN I BE MEAN TO MY CHARACTERS TODAY?" THEN, AS THE COMMERCIALS SAY, JUST DO IT.

The order in which you introduce your character's goals and conflicts isn't as important as the order in which you resolve them.

Haley Joel Osment's Cole was an astoundingly, well-crafted character, brought to life with gifted acting. As a result, Cole stole the show. But Bruce Willis's brilliant Dr. Malcolm Crowe was the main character, however you slice it. It was his goals that were most important. It was his struggle that kept us focused on what the writer wanted us to see. For your story to work right up to the last page, the main character's main conflict is the most important and should be resolved last.

My first rejection letter said that I needed to "dig deeper into the emotional lives of your characters and hence, create a more potent conflict between them." I had no idea what that meant until one of my critique partners read through my latest chapter and handed it back to me. "You like them too much," she said. "You're too nice to them." And *conflict* as a concept began to fall into place.

Conflict for your characters means you have to be mean.

However you define, think, talk, or write about conflict, make your characters suffer. And grow. And suffer some more. Make your characters *struggle* mightily, and you've mastered conflict.

Chapter Eight

Suspending Disbelief

ASSIGNMENT: *DIE HARD*

Once a writer gets past the inevitable form rejection letters based on something as nebulous and non-helpful as "the quality" of the writing, 92.7 percent of all other manuscript rejections are the direct result of credibility gaps.

Credibility gaps come down to one big question: Did you, the author, allow the audience—in this case, an editor or agent—to believe your story could be real?

The movie *Die Hard* is one long example of things that *could* have been story problems. But there are no credibility gaps, no chances for the audience to take back their willing suspension of disbelief, because the movie weaves seemingly inconsequential details into the story fabric in an incredible way. But before we get into what *Die Hard* did right, let's talk about rejection and the things you can control and the things you can't. Then, I'm going to show you examples of stories that didn't quite close the credibility gaps. After all, it's impossible to find examples of those in **Die Hard**.

When a reader reads your book, he knows you are lying to him. He bought it in the fiction section of the bookstore. He knows you made it all up. He wants to be told a story. So, logically, as God of the characters you've created, you should be able to do with them whatever you want. You're the master of your own fictional universe.

The screenwriters who wrote **Killer Klowns From Outer Space** must have believed that. You may find the movie on late, late night cable TV, but you'll have trouble finding the movie on anyone's list of all-time favorite movies. But, with a few word changes—the who and where—the listing in *TV Guide* could be interchanged with a program listing for **Alien**, the popular 1979 movie that is on many critics' lists of all-time favorite movies. One **Alien** program listing accurately described the movie with the blurb, "Space travelers battle killer aliens far away." The listing for **Killer Klowns From Outer Space** was, "Teenagers battle killer aliens in a small town." In the world where most of us live, teenagers sound more credible than space travelers, and a small town sounds much more realistic than a far away galaxy.

Even if the blurb had included a description of the aliens as either bug-like reptilians or clown-like with big teeth, it would be a toss up as to which would be more believable. How many of us actually know what an alien looks like? Our mass experience of the subject comes by way of fiction. Fortunately the **Killer Klowns** title—complete with the misspelling of clowns—warns away those who expect realism in their fiction.

Though readers usually turn to fiction as an escape from reality or for entertainment, when the vast majority of them read, they make a private, unspoken contract with the storyteller. They agree to invest money and time pretending the story is real. The reader willingly chooses to suspend disbelief. He trusts you, the author, to keep your part of the bargain.

THE AUTHOR'S PART OF THE BARGAIN

The instant you stop concerning yourself with what is real in your reader's world, the minute your character does something jarring, the second some "lucky coincidence" helps your protagonist out of a jam or disguises a big clue, the credibility gap breaks your side of the contract and screams: "The author made this up! It is a lie!"

A credibility gap is anything that keeps the reader/audience from believing that this story could happen in this way, in this time. A reader has to be convinced that this place *could* exist, that these characters *are likely* to be in this place, *doing* these things at this point in time because it is *inevitable* for the characters in the world the writer created.

The makers of **Alien** set the movie in the future and made it believable that technology could have advanced far enough to allow humans to travel to a far galaxy. They gave the characters completely human and understandable motivations, strengths, and weaknesses. The plot evolved in a logical way.

Overcoming one obstacle led to another larger obstacle, and to another and another. The characters' actions and reactions were true to the characters as the audience had come to know them. **Alien** worked because the writers blended all the essential elements of a story into one logical, believable, perfectly merged whole.

As an uncle of mine always used to say, "The devil is in the details."

BIG DETAILS? LITTLE DETAILS? WHICH DETAILS HAVE TO BE RIGHT?

What kind of details are we talking about? Individual words?

That's what writing teachers instruct. They're following the advice Mark Twain gave to a novice writer in 1888. He wrote, "The difference between the almost right word and the right word is really a large matter—it's the difference between the lightning bug and the lightning."

Most writers agree completely with the concept of getting every word right, because there is a huge difference between lightning bug and lightning. If you get those kinds of words wrong, you're in big trouble, and nobody will believe anything you write.

QUICK FIX:

REALISTIC DIALOGUE

UNREALISTIC DIALOGUE IS THE QUICKEST WAY TO MAKE YOUR STORY UNBELIEVABLE. BESIDES MAKING SURE IT SOUNDS LIKE REAL PEOPLE, MAKE CERTAIN YOUR DIALOGUE REFLECTS EACH CHARACTER'S BACKGROUND, EDUCATION, MINDSET, CAREER, ETC. READ IT AND REWORK IT AND REWORK IT AGAIN UNTIL EACH CHARACTER SOUNDS JUST LIKE THE UNIQUE PERSON HE SHOULD BE.

The words that cause most writers problems are things like "run" or "hurry" or "dash." I, personally, can account for whole hours spent changing one word to another that might be better, and then changing back to the original word again. After all, "ran" and "hurried" provide two different mental images, but both get the character where he's going faster than walking.

Your goal should be to plant the same image in your reader's head that you had in yours while writing a scene. That's the goal: an image implant. The more detailed the image you paint, the more likely the reader is to see the story the same way you did. That's why individual words are important.

Brian Lamb, the noted former host of C-Span's *Book Notes*, asked one of his guest authors if it was true that it took fifteen years for her to write her book. The author laughed. "Seventeen," she corrected sheepishly. That, I suspect, is how long it would take for most of us to get every single solitary word "right."

But few authors, especially those trying to make a living from their words, have seventeen years to write a book.

Though getting specific words right helps you implant an image in the reader's mind, getting story details right is vastly more important. If the story details are right, then individual words—like "ran" or "hurried"—don't have much power to skew a reader's perception.

How does this apply to suspending disbelief?

Those nitpicking details—the *right* details—cause the audience to feel that whatever happens next is as inevitable as night following day. It makes the impossible seem not only possible, but plausible.

DON'T TAKE IT PERSONALLY

For a moment, let's talk about the other 7.3 percent of rejections that aren't based on problems with the actual writing. They are often problems with the project as a whole.

The editor doesn't get past the first paragraph of the cover letter because he doesn't see how his company could—credibly and successfully—publish a children's picture book when they normally publish only non-fiction, do-it-yourself things like car repair manuals. Some writers do things as mind-boggling as submitting to completely wrong publishers, guaranteeing an instant, automatic rejection.

Your own personal taste will help you decide which markets are credible for you. Who is publishing the kind of books you like to read and want to write? Which publisher publishes stories similar to yours? Knowing the answers to those two questions solves that basic rejection problem.

Between the we-don't-publish-that-type-of-book rejection and the we-want-to-buy-your-book acceptance call, the line is usually much thinner and shaded with a lot more personal perception.

For example, a book written for young adult readers might be a bit grittier than the books that particular publisher usually markets. The editor might even love the story, but suspect it goes beyond what their target audience would accept. It's the publisher's job to know the market they're catering to. Guessing wrong can cost an editor his job. Crossing that thin, shadowy line in your manuscript might earn you the same, this-doesn't-fit-our-needs-at-this-time letter that you'd receive for submitting to the wrong market.

Say the editor does like your story. He does think it suits his audience. He buys your book. The next audience you'll face is the reader. Here is where it gets really personal. The stories a reader likes are a matter of personal taste.

Like millions of other moviegoers, I loved the original **Star Wars** movie. I identified with a common farm boy, Luke Skywalker, wanting to save the beautiful princess and, ultimately, the whole galaxy. His dreams and goals matched the dreams and goals of a lot of young and idealistic people. I could even identify with Chewbacca, though I couldn't understand him. When he said—in his own language—"Let's get the heck out of here," I fully bought into the sentiment. The world the filmmakers created, though not realistic if compared to the world I live in, was believable to me. It made sense. The characters had emotions I understood, motivated by reasons I also understood. The cast of characters held me on the edge of my seat until the end of the movie.

Unlike millions of other moviegoers, *The Matrix didn't* work for me. The rebels existed in dark and dingy places—without amenities I value—risking life, limb, and sanity to demolish a world that I found far more attractive than the one they wanted to establish. The premise—a painful reality is better than a pleasurable fantasy—created a huge credibility gap for me. I get plenty of the "painful reality." The longer I live, the more firmly I believe a "pleasurable fantasy" is ofttimes preferable. So, even though the bad guys in *The Matrix* didn't have my sympathy, the good guys didn't either. I couldn't connect with their goals. Their motivation was unfathomable. The fantasy was better than the reality the rebels were living. Disconnect. Done. Finished. I admired the special effects and watched that movie with detached indifference. And when my family went back for seconds—*The Matrix Reloaded*—I stayed home with a book.

Where and how far the reader is willing to go comes from his own personal tastes and his own personal realms of possibilities. You, the writer, can't do anything about those credibility gaps because they are personal.

Besides carefully targeting your market and making your characters' emotions, goals, and motivations universal, you can't do much about a reader's personal tastes. As a writer, you have to worry about the things you *can* control.

QUICK TIP:

THE PURPOSE-DRIVEN NOUN

STRIVE TO MAKE EVERY PERSON, PLACE, OR THING IN YOUR STORY HAVE A PURPOSE.

IF YOU FIND NOUNS THAT DON'T HAVE A PURPOSE, GIVE THEM ONE.

BETTER YET, USE A NOUN THAT *DOES* HAVE A PURPOSE.

GIVE A WALK-ON CHARACTER SOMETHING SIGNIFICANT TO DO OR SAY. (THE CO-PASSENGER AT THE BEGINNING OF *DIE HARD*.) PUT THE HOUSE WHERE YOUR HERO LIVES IN A LOCATION THAT CONTRIBUTES TO YOUR STORY IN SOME WAY. AS YOU PAINT YOUR WORD PICTURES, CHOOSE THE DETAILS IN YOUR PICTURE TO SHOW SOMETHING ADDITIONAL ABOUT THE CHARACTER OR TO FORESHADOW SOMETHING THAT WILL COME LATER. [THE FAMILY PICTURE IN HOLLY'S OFFICE DOES BOTH.]

THE READER'S REALITY

Credibility gaps that aren't personal come in as many shapes and sizes as there are stories. You know what I'm talking about. You've read and seen them. A ghost suddenly appears and the villain is so frightened he jumps off a cliff, saving the heroine from certain death. (Yes. That was in a real book by a real author whose books regularly hit bestseller lists.)

A character acts (or overreacts) in a way that hasn't been explained by the characterization thus far. In a manuscript I judged for a contest, the heroine of the story is out for her daily jog and comes across a rape in progress. She kicks butt—literally, she's a black belt in karate—scares the rapist away, comes to the aid of the victim, and then, when the policeman who comes to investigate touches her shoulder, she releases a blood-curdling scream and falls into a state of near catatonia.

The author usually tries to explain the credibility gap away. In the first example, the ghost had appeared a couple of times earlier in the book, at a garden many miles away. But there was no real explanation to tell me why the ghost

> ## QUICK TIP: 👈
>
> CHECK THE ESCAPE HATCH.
>
> *DON'T* GIVE YOUR CHARACTER OBSTACLES SHE LOGICALLY CAN'T GET OVER.
>
> *DO* LAY THE GROUNDWORK—AND SHOW IT BEING LAID—FOR HER TO GET OVER IT.
>
> FOR EXAMPLE: IF YOUR CHARACTER, WHO SEEMS TO BE A FINE, UPSTANDING CITIZEN, MUST ESCAPE FROM A ROOM BY PICKING A LOCK, SHOW HOW OR WHERE SHE ACQUIRED THAT SKILL IN AT LEAST ONE EARLIER SCENE.

appeared here and now, and nothing to foreshadow the villain's reaction when every other time the ghost appeared, the other characters who saw him reacted with a calm indifference.

In the second example, by reading a few more pages, I found that the jogger had been raped in the past. Okay. That explains a bit, but there was no explanation of the *extreme* reactions. From Super Heroine during the crime to Total Basket Case in sixty seconds or less? (It didn't work for me, but perhaps it was personal.)

Sometimes the explanation works enough to let us go on reading. But the damage is done.

If the groundwork hasn't been laid in advance to explain what is happening without a tossed in explanation after the fact, the reader now trusts you, the writer, a little less.

In another book, an author had scenes from a spirit's point of view scattered throughout the story. Suddenly, twenty pages from the end, thoughts in the spirit's third person point of view changed from *he* to *she*. In the author's explain-it-away paragraph, the ghost glibly reminded herself that, in life, she'd wished she was a man and had always thought of herself that way. The author broke the contract with me.

Way back at the beginning of the book, I suspected who the villain was and what was going on. When the he-spirit made his first appearance, I decided I was wrong. Then—twenty pages from the end of the book—I discovered the writer had written those scenes from a male's point of view for no other reason than to throw me off. I also knew that if the earlier scenes hadn't been written that way, the story would have been over by the end of the third chapter. No mystery. No story.

Instead of the satisfying conclusion I expected for my investment of time, I developed a refusal to suspend disbelief for that author ever again.

The difference between he and she is one letter. Yet one letter—one tiny detail the author chose intentionally—made all the difference.

But wait, you're saying. That wasn't a credibility gap. That was the author cheating! And you're partially right. But it was a detail the author chose instead of fixing the flaws in the story. And that's my point. You choose what will happen—and how it will be explained—in your story.

Usually you, as the reader, can count on an editor to protect you from outright cheating by the author. That's exactly why credibility gaps get manuscripts rejected.

But most credibility gaps aren't that blatant.

In the movie *The Rock*—written by David Weisburg, Douglas S. Cook, and Mark Rosner—Sean Connery's character, John Mason, is a political prisoner who has been "buried" in various high-security prisons for thirty years. While still in custody, Mason steals a Humvee and escapes from the government officials wanting to use him. He's in the midst of a big chase scene, and the phone rings in the Humvee.

Credibility Gap Alert: After several years of having a cell phone, I still don't know all the ins and outs of using it. Using a cell phone is a lot more complicated than using the pick-it-up-and-dial-while-staying-firmly-attached-to-one-spot instrument found only in buildings or booths, thirty years ago. Thirty years ago, 9-1-1 and 4-1-1 weren't an option. You dialed "0" to get an operator. Yet, Mason—after all those years in prison—knows, not only how to use that car phone, but whom and how to call for information. And he does it while racing through San Francisco traffic—after not having driven for three decades. On top of that, he's trying to elude the FBI guy (Nicholas Cage) chasing him in a Lamborghini. Then—while still envading the authorities and driving through traffic—he uses the phone to make a call. Yeah, right!

The movie was entertaining and fast paced enough that I slid right past the gap and kept watching. For those young enough to have always lived in the cell-phone age, it might not even cause a pause. And Mason's character was well established as a brilliant man so, if not totally believable, the credibility gap was somewhat forgivable.

It is much easier to put a book down. That's why it's important to learn to recognize credibility gaps and to know how to fix them.

Seeing problems in your own work is sometimes next to impossible. As the author you know what is *supposed* to be there. It's like reading a page again and again for spelling errors, and not catching that you've left out a word or typed "us" instead of "use." Your eyes read the word "use" or fill in the missing blank because your mind tells them what is supposed to be there. It's similar to the reason things go awry when we read body language or make a faulty judgment about a first impression. We see things that aren't there—or things that are—partially based on our expectations.

Writers tend to do the same thing in their stories. You've spent lots of time with this story and character. You've thought long and hard about the

QUICK FIX:

IF YOUR MANUSCRIPT HAS A PROBLEM . . .

OR EVEN IF YOU DON'T KNOW IT HAS A PROBLEM . . . FIND A GOOD CRITIQUE GROUP OR PARTNER. SEE PAGE 224 FOR SUGGESTIONS ON FINDING ONE.

YOU'LL LEARN FASTER BY CRITIQUING SOMEONE ELSES WORK.. YOUR PARTNER WILL LEARN BY CRITIQUING YOURS.

characters, strengths and weaknesses. You know what motivates the character. You know why he chooses to go through the alley rather than taking the route most people would travel. Will the reader know? Is the reason there, on paper? Did something the character has done thus far—not just in your mind but on the page—make the reason for the choice clear?

The only way to tell is to have a trusted reader read it. That's why many authors swear by critique groups. If two or three people see something you think is or isn't there, count on it. They're right. Make sure the reason is on paper, the way you intended it to be, not just in your imagination. Make sure your hero didn't choose to walk through the alley because it was convenient for you, the author.

Recognizing problems comes with practice. So practice. Read and watch a lot of stories, both good and bad. When something jars you even slightly, examine it. Figure out why there's a problem and how it could have been fixed.

CREATING INEVITABILITY

When planning a book, most authors have the big scenes in mind: pivotal points in the plot, growth markers for the characters, the major obstacles, all the things we've talked about so far. The threads that tie those different story elements together—the right small details and small scenes—are just as important.

Details in those scenes connect everything and make the reader feel certainty and inevitability.

Inevitability lies in consistency and logic. Making sense of the senseless depends strongly on consistency. You, the author, may play God and change the world to suit your story. But you have to set up the parameters you'll work in and remain consistent within that framework.

In the movie *Heart and Souls*, for example, we're living in the real world but experiencing it through the viewpoint of ghosts—something most of us aren't familiar with.

There were very defined things those ghosts could and couldn't do. Just as the world we live in has rules, the world that the screenwriters Gregory Hansen, Erik Hansen, Brent Maddock, and S.S. Wilson created for the souls had rules, too. The ghosts can't get more than fifteen feet away from the person their souls are attached to. The story never lets them stray from that basic rule.

When it rains, the ghosts don't get wet. Though they can't touch someone who is living, they can take over the body of the character they are attached to. The writers established rules for their "souls" and then stuck to them. They were consistent with the physical rules, right up until the end. Once the audience knows your rules, even if you are writing some fantasy world, they'll hang around unless you break them.

> **QUICK TIP:**
>
> CONSISTENCY
>
> MAKE RULES FOR YOUR PHYSICAL, MENTAL AND EMOTIONAL WORLD, THEN STICK TO THEM.

But consistency doesn't end with the physical, mental, or emotional realm you've created. Consistency also must apply to every other aspect of your story, including the subtle contract you've made with the reader.

Promises must be consistently kept.

When the four people die at the beginning of the movie, their souls attached to a living person—in their case, all four of them attach to the same baby as it is born. The souls are allowed to stay in the earthly world so they can have ". . . the opportunity to resolve the one thing you would have done had your life not been cut short by some idiot." (In other words, it wasn't their time to die so they have the opportunity to tie up some loose ends.)

At the end of *Heart and Souls*, Julia, one of the souls (played by Kyra Sedgwick), doesn't get to resolve her problem. She doesn't get her opportunity to tell the fiancé she rejected before she died that she loved him. The fiancé, John, has died since her own demise.

Credibility Gap Alert! Julia suddenly realizes she's been left behind in this ghostly purgatory, not to resolve her own loose ends, but to keep Thomas Reilly, the hero played by Robert Downey Jr., from making the same mistakes she did.

> **QUICK FIX:**
>
> FIND A DIFFERENT WAY TO SOLVE A PROBLEM.
>
> IF A PROBLEM CAN'T BE RESOLVED LOGICALLY OR AN OBSTACLE CAN'T BE OVERCOME IN A WAY THAT MAKES SENSE, MAKE THE PROBLEM OR OBSTACLE SMALLER.
>
> EXAMPLE: IF YOU CAN'T FIND A LOGICAL REASON FOR YOUR FINE, UPSTANDING CITIZEN TO KNOW HOW TO PICK LOCKS SO HE CAN ESCAPE THE ROOM, MAKE THE DOOR ONE HE CAN TAKE OFF THE HINGES WITH SOMETHING HE FINDS IN THE ROOM.

The first and most important problem with this infamous explanation is that if the souls had resolved things immediately following their deaths—as they were supposed to but didn't, because someone forgot to tell them—Thomas, the baby, wouldn't have been old enough to help them as he was supposed to or to benefit from Julia's experience. He wouldn't have learned a thing from her mistakes.

The writers probably congratulated themselves for the unexpected twist. Julia's realization does lead to the movie's final resolution, but it isn't very satisfying for the veiwer.

QUICK FIX:

IF A SCENE DOESN'T WORK . . . ONE POSSIBLE CAUSE? THE LOGIC IS FLAWED. LOGIC IS DEFINED BY THE WORDS: COHERENT, CONSISTENT, PROBABLE, SOUND, COGENT, PERTINENT, GERMANE, LEGITIMATE, RATIONAL, PERCEPTIVE, REASONABLE, AND SENSIBLE. IF YOU CAN'T IDENTIFY ANY PREVIOUS SCENES WITH ELEMENTS, DETAILS, ACTIONS, OR REACTIONS THAT LED TO THIS MOMENT, EITHER CHANGE THIS SCENE OR ADD AND STRENGTHEN THE DETAILS IN EARLIER SCENES TO MAKE THIS SCENE COHERENT, CONSISTENT, PROBABLE, PERTINENT, REASONABLE . . . ETC.

I believe the inconsistency could have been fixed with one tiny line of dialogue. Julia could have realized, "John's waiting for me," and excitedly, happily, prepared to climb on the bus to the hereafter. (See the movie. You'll know exactly what I mean.) The audience would have known that she would soon have her opportunity to tell the fiancé she'd rejected that she really loved him. Even though we wouldn't actually see her resolution, it would have been satisfying to know that that she would get it finally.

Then she could have realized that she could keep Thomas from making the same mistakes she had made. That realization coming after we knew she would get to take care of what she needed to resolve, that one tiny change, would have added an additional and extremely satisfying element to the story. That fix would have provided a divine reason for the devilish blunder that kept the souls in limbo for twenty-six years. It could have been an "ah-ha" moment for Julia *and* the audience. Her realization could have been, "Ah-ha! *Now* I understand why we were kept hanging around all these years, instead of resolving our problems right after our deaths, as was intended. I was supposed to be here to make sure you didn't make the same mistakes I did." It would have untangled one more loose thread and woven it nicely into the whole cloth of the story. There wouldn't have been the slightest credibility gap.

I discovered the movie at the video store and loved it enough to dig until I found a copy to buy. But I had never heard of it before then. I've always suspected the movie would have been much more successful had the audience received the satisfying resolution it expected and was promised. That one flaw—Julia not getting her resolution and the audience not getting what was promised—kept a fun, heartwarming, and very entertaining movie from being as good as it could have been. That inconsistency, the unkept promise so near to the end, was a letdown.

A big difference between real life and good fiction is that fiction must be logical.

In real life the bad guys kill old ladies for reasons no one ever figures out. In the movie *Don't Say A Word*, bad guys kill an old lady, but we're provided with logic that explains it. Her apartment is convenient for spying on the psychiatrist whose daughter they've kidnapped.

In real life one person can fall in love with another for no apparent or understandable reason. The fictional couple cannot fall in love simply because it's convenient for the writer because he's writing a romance. For fiction to work, the couple must have a logical reason the audience can recognize.

In *How to Lose a Guy in 10 Days*, Matthew McConaughey's character sticks with Kate Hudson's character much, much longer than any other sane, sensible person would stick around. But we understand it. They both have selfish, professional reasons for staying together. The screenwriters—Kristen Buckley, Brian Regan, and Burr Steers—gave us the logical reasons, one after another, right up front.

In the movie *My Cousin Vinny*, several things created logic gaps for me. The largest was Vinny's (Joe Pesci) lack of knowledge about disclosure. In real life, even if it took fifty tries to pass the bar exam, could a lawyer really pass at all without knowing such an elementary thing? I know about it just from watching movies, reading books, and watching the news and current events. How could Vinny have missed it?

Comedies seem to have a bit more leeway in the logic department. But even then, there's a *logical* reason why. The audience knows, going in, that they are going to see the world from a comic slant. The logic of a comic character might be a little twisted or different. The audience logically grants the writer a bit more latitude in the unspoken contract with the author.

Every scene has to have details that paint a picture for the reader. Why not use your details to show consistency and develop your story logic? Sometimes that's called foreshadowing. And it's as simple as using every opportunity your story provides you.

QUICK TIP:

FORESHADOWING

PLANT MARKERS OR CONNECTIONS. WATCH FOR OPPORTUNITIES TO LAY THEM ALONG THE WAY. OR ADD THEM LATER.

FORESHADOWING: GETTING THE DETAILS RIGHT

Many people think *foreshadowing* means dropping hints of things-to-come, but that doesn't begin to cover what foreshadowing can and should do. Foreshadowing that is well executed connects things and keeps them consistent. Skillful foreshadowing lets the reader tie together cause and effect.

DOING IT RIGHT

Jeb Stuart and Steven E. de Sousa—the screenwriters of **Die Hard**, based on the novel *Nothing Lasts Forever* by Roderick Thorp—didn't put in a single unnecessary scene, line of dialogue, or detail. They didn't overlook any opportunity to let many scenes do double and even triple duty. Seemingly unimportant things early in the movie foreshadow and have major impact later.

From the beginning the viewers see markers that seem insignificant leading to other seemingly insignificant markers leading to others. Then when something happens we have a very clear picture from mentally connecting dots the writers gave us.

When we first meet Sgt. Powell, the cop played by Reginald Veljohnson, he's in a convenience store buying Twinkies (the writers start with a stereotype and build on it.) When he defends his purchase to the smart aleck clerk by saying they are for his pregnant wife, we assume it's just that. A defense. That marker leads to a later, casual conversation with Bruce Willis's character, John McClane, about their children someday playing together, and that later ties into a conversation about the child Al shot, which leads to the question of whether Al could ever shoot a gun at anyone again. That statement leaves a marker that notches up an additional moment of tension at the end when the last bad guy storms out the door, intent on finally killing McClane. Will Al be able or unable to draw his weapon and shoot?

In the first ten minutes of the movie, I counted twenty-four different markers that were laid. Each led to later events that surprised yet left the audience feeling they "should have seen it coming." Inevitability! See how many markers you can count. When you're adding details to create a clear picture, think of ways you can also use those details as markers. For example, say your laid-back protagonist will eventually go off the deep end with a mechanic later in your story. Give your hero's apartment a white carpet when you're establishing *place*. Later the mechanic can leave an oily footprint on that carpet when he's bringing back the hero's car. When the blowup comes even later, don't let it rest on one big thing. Make it a build up of small things the reader can see.

If your normally upbeat heroine is going to be discouraged and down by the end of the day, make the first thing she sees out the window in the morning a blah and foggy day. You can actively choose details that give your story extra dimension and create a sense of inevitability.

WORKING BACKWARD

If you were recounting the plot of *Die Hard* to a friend, when you got to the part about how the bad guy gets back his all-important blasting caps toward the end, you'd probably be doing some backtracking for extra explanations. "Why is the good guy, a New York cop who is a guest at a company holiday party in California, running around this upscale high-rise office building without his shoes?" your friend would want to know. Oh, yeah. That little detail didn't seem so important in the beginning did it?

Bruce Willis's character, John McClane, is first introduced to the viewer on a plane—and obviously not liking it much. His seat companion—someone we never see or hear from again—gives him some advice about dealing with jet lag: "Take off your shoes and fist your toes in the carpet."

When John follows the advice and takes off his shoes, we don't think it is strange because he is so obviously trying to feel "grounded" in what is obviously a foreign and uncomfortable environment. When the gunfire starts, he has a reason—one we might think is strange but one we understand—to be barefoot.

We're not surprised when the pursued John gripes because his first casualty has small feet (which means he can't appropriate the victim's shoes for himself.) At this point, we think this is just a small obstacle the character has to deal with, a quirky little detail that adds interest and an occasional bit of humor to release some of the tension.

When John finally meets Hans Gruber (Alan Rickman) face-to-face, they actually meet face-to-feet. Hans lands at John's feet and can't help noticing that John is barefoot. Hans uses the knowledge against John a short time later. He thinks he has John McClane trapped and tells his associate, "Shoot the glass," and we suddenly see all the connections.

We're relieved a few minutes later to see John in the bathroom, tweezing glass from his feet. But the obstacle of broken glass does get Hans his blasting caps back. That seemingly meaningless throwaway line of dialogue—"Take off your shoes and fist your toes"—is actually a crucial element of the story.

We don't know how the writer originally conceived the idea of having John barefoot. Did the idea come early in the process? Did it come later, when he was trying to figure out how Hans Gruber would get his blasting caps back?

One could picture the author *working backward*. I see him stewing over the pivotal plot point where Hans Gruber *has* to get the blasting caps back. The bad guys *can't* catch John yet. That development would completely change the story he has planned. In the picture in his mind, John is trapped in a glassed-in room. He sees John escaping through a blizzard of shattering glass. And the light bulb goes off. "Ohhh, wouldn't it be great if he were barefoot?"

And the author could have worked backward from there. Why would he have his shoes off? At what point in the story would he take them off?

In my experience, some of the best developments come late in the writing process. They work because the author then backs up and figures out how to seed a development earlier in the text, so the reader won't think, "Yeah, right! Lucky coincidence." When the event happens, the author has laid the groundwork to make the event seem inevitable.

Making the details of a story as interwoven and perfectly shaped into a pleasing pattern as the writers did with **Die Hard** is tough. Isn't it a relief to know that some of the elements—the small details—can be added later to fine-tune your story?

Many authors write their stories in layers. They get the essentials down and then expand and add details over multiple run-throughs of the manuscript.

GIFTS

Let's look at another, seemingly unimportant detail: When we meet Holly (Bonnie Bedelia) we learn very shortly that Holly goes by her maiden name— Gennaro—at work. Holly doesn't know what to expect when or if she sees her estranged husband. She's not sure he's coming for Christmas, let alone whether he'll stay with her and their children at her house. She looks at the family portrait she has sitting behind her desk and then lowers it, face-down, to the table. What we see is an outward gesture of her frustration and ambiguous feelings about her personal life. We see it as just a showing bit of characterization. At that point in the story, we don't know the importance of that small, telling incident.

Later, when the viewer does find out how lucky it was that the picture wasn't showing—Hans would have put the pieces together more quickly and would have used Holly to get John to cooperate—we don't consider the picture lying face down on the table a coincidence. We know how it happened. We know *why* she lowered it.

Yet how often do you see, both in books and movies, an important development hinging on some lucky coincidence—like a bad guy, in the book discussed earlier, seeing the ghost and jumping off a cliff.

> **QUICK TIP:**
>
> WRITE REGULARLY.
>
> WRITERS WHO WRITE ON A CONSISTENT SCHEDULE—REGULARLY, IF NOT DAILY—GET MORE GIFTS FROM THEIR SUBCONSCIOUS. YOUR SUBCONSCIOUS WON'T WORK ON SOMETHING IF YOU AREN'T CONSCIOUSLY WORKING ON IT AT SOME POINT, TOO.

In *Die Hard*, the writers could have chosen to show the picture being moved and even laid face-down on the table by the janitorial staff cleaning the building. A distraction could interrupt the cleaner before he got the chance to move the picture back to its former, upright location. It would have made the incident more significant and called more attention to the detail, but it would have worked. However it wouldn't have been as effective as the scene with Holly.

The first and most important reason for the scene to exist at all is to introduce us to Holly. The writer wrote a scene to show her frustration with her marriage and her personal relationship with John. Her gesture, placing the photograph face-down, probably happened automatically as he wrote the scene, using that to capture her character's frustration. Later—or maybe even as soon as it was written—he may have realized how much her action helped the story.

Often, while you're writing, you add a detail with nothing more in mind than painting a clearer picture or revealing character. Your fingers type it in. It seems to fit, but you wonder where the small item came from in the first place. One of the best gifts you can give yourself as a writer is to learn to trust your subconscious. Leave in the details that cause you to question, "Where'd that come from?"

You may end up taking some of these details out in the revision process. But sometimes you get to a point in your story and realize why your sub-conscious had you put it there in the first place. That detail or quirk in your character or the peculiar way someone says a line of dialogue foreshadows something in a way you didn't think about in the planning stages. If you let it, your subconscious does all kinds of favors for you. When your subconscious gives you a gift, accept it.

What if the picture had just been lying face-down on the credenza with no explanation whatsoever? Whether it's sheer oversight or no one thinks a minor detail is important, writers get by with that sort of thing all the time. You'll even find authors who argue that they don't want to insult the intelligence of the reader by explaining "too much." Surely the reader gets that the character is confused and frustrated by her relationship. Why would the reader be surprised that Holly can't bear to look at her family's portrait? Just show the picture face-down. Let the reader draw *some* conclusions for themselves. Why not?

Go right back to that contract you've made with the reader. By the very act of submitting the book for publication, you have promised to do your best to keep the reader's reality intact. Forcing the reader to draw his own conclusions leaves the door open for a far different interpretation of events than you intended. Remember the goal: the image implant.

If you don't work toward that goal, you leave the door open for the reader to think, "Yeah, right. Lucky coincidence." Technically, almost everything in a story is a lucky coincidence. Wasn't it convenient that Hans and his gang show up on the same day John does? Isn't it convenient that Holly looked at the picture on this day, rather than a different one? The reader gives you those "lucky coincidences" when he suspends disbelief. After all, that situation *is* the story. The point is that if the reader knows the reason why the little things happen—John's coming for Christmas, and Holly is feeling stressed because of his possible visit—the picture incident doesn't seem like a convenience for the writer. It's often the difference between a story you want to read or see again—one that is seamless and flawless—and one that is eminently forgettable.

A flawed story makes the author eminently forgettable, too. The reader won't be anxiously seeking out your next book in the bookstore.

Study how threads are woven together; how subtly they come back later to form an intricate pattern; how the echoes advance the story, then advance the story even more.

Study the movie *Holes*. In it, three different story lines come together in a fun and wonderful way. Basically a kids' movie, it is almost a perfect movie to study because it is so simple and straightforward. If you want complexity and serious practice picking out the pieces that make a story work, watch *The Usual Suspects*, and 1973's Academy Award choice for Best Picture of the Year, *The Sting*. You might have to watch them several times, but you'll understand why their screenwriters won the Oscar.

GETTING AWAY WITH DOING IT WRONG

Making the details work with you to tell your story is perhaps the most important part of a writer's job. What if you find holes, inconsistencies, and loose details upon review, but don't come up with any lightning bolt "barefoot" ideas to fix them? They will jolt your readers. So how do you fix them?

In *While You Were Sleeping*, one of the most memorable scenes is the ice scene where Jack and Lucy are slipping and sliding around, right into each other's arms. The scene is a pivotal one, one that confirms the growing romantic awareness between Jack and Lucy and provides a major turning point.

About the sixth or seventh time I watched the movie, I noticed that there was really no reason for them to be slipping and sliding around.

Where had the ice come from? Wasn't Lucy hurrying—almost running—over that same section of sidewalk only that morning? Had it rained? Snowed?

Rewind and rewatch. Sure enough, Lucy had dashed across that same, very dry sidewalk that very morning to avoid Joe Jr. It hadn't rained or snowed. Though Joe Jr. had been working on his car, he hadn't been washing it and dumping loads of water on the sidewalk. He'd been checking his oil or doing something under the hood. The sidewalks were clear of snow.

Minutes before Jack and Lucy are slipping and sliding around on the ice, they walk across a bridge, not slipping and sliding, not even watching for icy patches. We all know from driving signs that a bridge is more likely to accumulate moisture and freeze than a cleared sidewalk in a grassy area.

How did the director/writers/someone convince me that I shouldn't give this scene a second thought the first six times I watched it? What caused me to suspend disbelief and not question what I know of reality?

MY REALITY

I live in a wintry state. That's my reality. Yes, sometimes snow melts during the day and refreezes at night. But my reality says that if the walks are shoveled clean, there is very little chance that even a lot of melted snow is going to layer two inches of ice on a flat sidewalk. Most of the melting ice is going to seep directly into the ground as it slowly melts. So how did I not question that scene?

Someone planted an image or thought in my mind.

Check the opening scenes played behind the credits at the beginning of the movie. You'll see a skater fall flat on the ice. Later, another seemingly unimportant detail is used as a transition to the beginning of a new day. A newspaper boy throws a paper and hits an icy spot on the sidewalk at the same time. He goes flying—and a very specific image is set in our subconscious. People fall on ice. Icy patches can be random.

Two tiny, random details, yet they planted an image that allowed the writers to get away with a pivotal scene without having the audience—even those of us from wintry states—question reality. Without those seemingly inconsequential incidents, would I have been drawn from the story to wonder why they were slipping and sliding on ice that wasn't there earlier? I

can't say for certain because I never saw it without those incidents, but I'd bet money I'd question it and be thrown out of the story for at least a moment.

The first time something happens, it's happenstance.

The second time something happens, it is coincidence.

The third time something happens, it proves a point.

And that is the Rule of Three.

I don't know where the rule came from. It's used in math, science, art, architecture, military strategy, public speaking, religion, and about anything else you can name. According to Web sites on the subject, a pattern can be called a pattern only if it has been applied to or found in a real-world situation at least three times.

I first heard the Rule of Three applied to writing by an editor. I've had several conversations with other authors who questioned why various editors asked the authors to add things in revisions that made them feel like they were hitting the readers over the head with something. "Do they think our readers are stupid?" someone usually asked. I get it now! The authors aren't explaining things; they're reinforcing the reality of the situation.

Perhaps Lewis Carroll explains it best in his poem, "The Hunting of the Snark": *"What I tell you three times is true."*

Applying the Rule of Three seems to produce magic. It helps suspend disbelief.

In *Spider-man* Peter Parker doesn't accept that he's a changed man until unexpected things happen to him three times. Then he's a believer—and the audience is right there believing with him. Review all the movies we've watched. You'll find the Rule of Three running through all of them.

In *The Sixth Sense*, before Cole reveals that he sees dead people, though he accepts Malcolm reluctantly, he does accept and interact with him—three times. The first time, Cole asks Malcolm if he's a good doctor. The second time, he tells him, "You're nice, but you can't help me." The third time, he delights in Malcolm's assurance that he isn't a "freak." Contrast that with the three times after the revelation that he sees dead people. His reaction to those ghosts is different—terrified—than any of his reactions to Malcolm's presence. The Rule of Three helps keep the secert plot twist.

When you absolutely cannot fix a credibility gap with consistency, logic, laying markers, or by working backward—and when your subconscious hasn't come up with any spectacular surprises—remember the Rule of Three.

FACT OR FICTION?

Now, go back and read the first paragraph of this chapter. I'm betting you believed I knew what I was talking about when you read the statistic about 92.7 percent of rejections. I made it up. However I've seen enough rejections—my own and others—that I'd be willing to bet the figure is close to true.

You may have stopped to think, "How does she know that?" You may have questioned where the statistic came from. But you're still reading this chapter. Not knowing where I got that tidbit didn't stop you from accepting that I was telling you something factual. Why? Several reasons.

One: You willfully suspended disbelief. You started trusting me to know what I was talking about the minute you plunked down your money for this book and gave me your time.

Two: I helped you keep suspending disbelief by being consistent and logical. I didn't equivocate. I stated it flatly, as if it were true. I used a

solid, factual-sounding specific number and made the details sound authentic. Had I used the word "most" rather than a percentage, you might have questioned my statement. "Most" is vague. "Most" might have made you wonder where I got it. At the very least, "most" would have left it up to your own concept to decide what "most" is. Just over half? Almost all? Two thirds? Solid and specific is the nitpicky kind of detail you plant when you work backward.

Three: I referred to it three times.

Those are the kinds of details that make fiction seem like fact—getting the details right. That's how you escape having credibility gaps. Getting the details right lets your reader sit back, relax, and happily enjoy your made-up story.

Chapter Nine

Five-Star Plotting

ASSIGNMENT: *BRIDGET JONES'S DIARY*

Writers often say they're talking about the plot of their book when what they are really talking about is their story: the characters and their goals, obstacles, and conflicts.

Most people (including writers) use the words *plot* and *story* interchangeably, but if you look up the word plot in the dictionary, you'll find that nothing in the definition resembles characters, goals, obstacles, or conflict. Every definition of the word "plot" has to do with planning, marking off, or mapping. Even the part of the definition that refers specifically to novels and books specifies that plot is a *plan* of action. In other words, plot is a *blueprint* for your story.

Plotting was a struggle for me. It suddenly made sense when I realized that story and plot were *not* the same thing.

Premise, characterization, goals, character growth, conflict—all the things we've discussed up until now—are about the story. Plotting is about structure. Plotting answers the question: How are you going to put all of those elements together? It's how the story unfolds. It's the answer to "What happens next?"

Plot is your plan of action—the *action* being how you are going to tell the story.

Writing a story without structuring the elements according to a plan would be like hoping to end up with a house if you decided to just throw all the pieces you needed—the lumber, cement, shingles, doors, windows, etc.— together without a blueprint. You might end up with something that resembles a house. It might have everything most people would consider necessary for a house to have. But it certainly wouldn't be your dream home. And it definitely would not be the best house it could be.

Plotting isn't about what elements go into a scene in general—although that is part of it. It's about what goes into an early scene in your story versus what belongs in the later ones. It is about which scene belongs where to make the story the best it can be. It's fitting the pieces together. What goes into the scene is only applicable in the plotting process if you're missing an essential part of something you need to make your story strong. (Back to the analogy of the house: Your foundation could look like a foundation, but it would be pretty weak if you forgot to put rebar in the cement in all the necessary places.)

WHAT'S DRIVING THE STORY?

But before we get too far into a discussion of structure, we need to talk about the difference between a character-driven plot and an action-driven plot.

A character-driven plot is more about the growth of the characters than about the action that causes the growth. In a character-driven story the character is more interesting than the action. The reader focuses on how the character reacts to the action taking place. Though **Thelma and Louise** has plenty of action, the characters, their motivation, and the decisions and choices those characters make are what keeps the audience fascinated. The way the characters act or react, and the choices they make regarding whatever action is taking place are what we remember. The character-driven story begins with the character recognizing some problem he faces or something that he needs to change. Then he acts. The character's actions advance the story.

In an action-driven plot, the character usually *reacts* to a happening—a situation or event—that has taken place. An action-driven plot keeps an audience enthralled with the excitement of the events that are unfolding. You turn the pages—or wait to go get popcorn—because you don't want to miss whatever exciting event is going to happen next. The characters are still extremely important because they keep us caring about the action, but we aren't glued to our seats because we're waiting to see what emotion the hero feels about the situation. We're glued to our seats to see if the character can measure up to the challenge and respond adequately to the next physical explosion or rolling boulder or whatever event they face. **Raiders of the Lost Ark** is a prime example of a story propelled by action. Though Indiana Jones (Harrison Ford) is a fascinating and well-built character, what we remember first is the nonstop action and various physical obstacles he faces. (And yes, we remember the humor he faces them with, but even then it is part of his reaction to the situation.)

Genre may help decide whether your story is action- or character-driven.

A movie or book billed as an action-adventure obviously leans toward a story driven by action. Many classic mysteries are also driven by action. A body is discovered, and then for whatever motive, the hero or heroine leaps into action to figure out what happened and who did it.

Horror and romance tend to be character-driven. (Horror, you ask? Think *Alien*.) The good horror stories often pivot around the humans who respond to the challenge of defeating the monster, not the actual monstrous events. Science fiction and suspense seem to be a mix of stories that are action-oriented and those that are character-driven. You can often tell whether a story is action-driven or character-driven based on what happens first. Are you introduced to the characters first (*Alien*), or does the story start with action (*True Lies*)?

Genre doesn't dictate which kind of plot you have. You'll find action-driven plots in romance and character-driven plots in mystery or action-adventure. If you're not sure whether to classify a story as action-driven or character-driven, consider what comes to mind first when you begin to play with an idea for a particular story. Do you think about the action or the character? It's a good clue. When you are considering ideas for your story, which most often spring to mind? Specific events or how the character is going to react if those events happen?

Is knowing which kind of story you have important? Since I had three books published before I really considered whether my stories were more character-oriented than action-oriented, it must not be crucial. But knowing will help you make decisions about structure and assist you in pacing. And it will help you add to or balance the elements you need to create a nice mixture of both. Writers tend to find their ideas and shape their stories based on one way of thinking or the other.

When I begin writing a book, the main character almost always takes shape in my mind first. The character comes complete with a specific problem he will face, but then I develop situations that will challenge him, and fine-tune other characters who will, in some way, be at odds with the main character, ensuring lots of conflict and struggle. More often than not, I shape the events around making the character grow.

But one of my novels didn't work that way. When I began it—the one romantic suspense novel I've written thus far—I woke up one day with several fully-formed events and incidents in mind. I had to build characters that would be challenged by the events and grow to meet them. That was a rare occurrence for me. I imagine it would be uncommon for a more action-oriented writer to find herself suddenly coming up with character-driven story ideas. But I know it happens. I've even seen writers start out as more character-driven writers and gradually become more action-oriented, and vice versa. Part of that is growth as a writer. We learn to diversify as we get better.

The ideal finished product is a medley of exciting action with fully developed characters. Most of the movies we've examined here are a balanced combination of the two. The wonderful mix makes them worthy of examination for that very reason. It also explains one of the reasons they were so successful at the box office.

Readers—and moviegoers—love a story with a strong emphasis on both character *and* action. While some people prefer action and one exhilarating happening after another, others prefer stories in which the characters and their growth are of primary importance. A well-structured story that has a nice mix of both attracts audiences *and* provides a foundation for a block-buster. And everyone's happy!

There isn't a standard combination of character or action, no correct formula, because every story is unique. So do not be intimidated thinking you have to reach an ideal. There is no such thing. As with every element we've discussed, it all depends on your story. Plotting—mapping out your story—helps you find the correct blend for your story.

BUILDING A STORY

To qualify as a story, yours must have a beginning, a middle, and an end. The beginning and end are the easy parts. Most writers have those in mind when they get the kernel of the idea. They might not know exactly *where* to start. And they might not know exactly *what* will happen at the end. But they do know how it will end. The protagonist will either be defeated by or triumph over the problem. Most authors know which it's going to be when the idea forms in their minds. The struggle to determine the outcome—whether the hero will win or lose—is the middle.

Let's dissect the pieces that, when strung together, make up the plot: the scenes. In comparing plotting with building a house, a scene is like an individual room of the house. Different rooms have different purposes, each distinct and separate from the other. Some of those rooms are public and lend themselves to activity and gathering: the kitchen and dining and living rooms for example. Others, like bedrooms and bathrooms, are meant for privacy and rest and refuge. They all flow together, one after another. The doorway through which you leave one room leads into another.

Scenes compare nicely to that. They flow together, one leading to another. They are distinct and separate. There are also two types of scenes and two purposes: one type of scene is where things happen (action), and the other is where the character reflects on what has happened (reaction), regroups, and decides his next course of action.

SCENES AND SEQUELS

Dwight Swain, in his book *Techniques of the Selling Writer* (a great addition to any writer's library), calls the two types of scenes Scene and Sequel.

QUICK FIX:

IF YOUR STORY IS TOO INTROSPECTIVE...

CONSIDER GIVING YOUR CHARACTER A FRIEND / ROOMMATE / CO-WORKER / BROTHER TO TALK TO. OR TRY TO SET SEQUEL SCENES WHERE THERE WILL BE OTHER PEOPLE. OR MOVE YOUR CHARACTER TO SUCH A PLACE FOR THE REFLECTIVE SCENES. IF ALL ELSE FAILS, ORDER YOUR CHARACTER A PIZZA.

Both types of scenes are "scenes" in the broad sense of the word. They both are segments of the overall story. The difference between the two is their purpose. A Scene (we'll capitalize the two to distinguish "scene" in general from either the Scene or a Sequel, the two distinct types of scenes we're talking about here) is action, literal or metaphorical, as in something-happening-to-advance-the-story. A Sequel is reflective. The character takes-a-breather-to-see-where-she-stands in this segment of the story.

Both Scenes and Sequels have a beginning, a middle, and an end, just like your big story. And that is exactly what the scenes are: tiny little stories.

The beginning of any Scene is like the beginning of the overall story. The character acts on a decision, establishes a goal, and sets things into motion. The middle of a Scene is where we see the character trying to achieve that goal. The end of the scene is the resolution of that tiny little story.

Let's look at a Sequel from the movie **Bridget Jones's Diary** where Bridget (Renée Zellweger) looks at her calendar at the end of a very bad day and sees that she is committed to go to dinner with "smug married couples." Her decision to go starts the next Scene.

In the beginning of the Scene your character takes action. Bridget goes to the dinner with the aforementioned couples. Her goal for this scene is to get through it with a modicum of dignity intact.

The middle of the Scene consists of seeing how the character handles—or doesn't handle—the action she has taken. The middle of the scene is about conflict, your character's struggle. Bridget's tired of being the "odd woman out." She's already had a horrible day, and she has to stay on her toes to dodge the slings and arrows her dinner companions all seem intent on aiming at her. She isn't handling the problem—smug married couples—especially well. She's finally about to escape.

The Scene ends with a resolution. She either wins or loses her struggle. In this case a disheartened Bridget feels she has definitely lost this struggle. Then Mark Darcy follows her out—she thinks to insult her—and instead, tells her, "I like you, just the way you are." In the small sense of this tiny little story, this resolves her problem by reassuring her it doesn't matter that she isn't part of the club of

QUICK TIP:

A STORY CHAIN . . .

IS A USEFUL TOOL FOR MAPPING OUT YOUR STORY. LIST AND LINK THE MAIN CHARACTER'S ACTION AND REACTIONS FOR A CHARACTER-DRIVEN STORY; LIST OR LINK THE CAUSES AND EFFECTS OF AN ACTION-DRIVEN STORY. START WITH THE OPENING SCENE AND THINK THROUGH YOUR STORY, LISTING THE MAJOR ACTIONS / REACTIONS OR CAUSES/EFFECTS. IT WILL HELP YOU SHAPE YOUR SCENES INTO A LOGICAL ORDER. (FIND A SAMPLE AND A PRINTABLE BLANK FORM AT WWW.LIGHTSCAMERAFICTION.COM] "smug married couples"—he likes her anyway.

In the large sense of the rest of the story, a Scene advances the story and takes it to a new level. In this Scene Bridget has attracted the notice of Mark Darcy and is revising her previous, unflattering opinion of him.

The end of the Scene is the door into the Sequel where the character reacts to what has happened in the Scene. In the Sequel, the character evaluates where that leaves her and decides how she will deal with whatever just happened. The decision leads into the next Scene.

The beginning of the Sequel is about reaction. It shows the character's response to the action of the Scene: Bridget is dazed by Mark's comments. She gathers her friends to tell them about the Scene.

In the middle of the Sequel, the character evaluates and deals with what has happened: Bridget and her friends analyze Mark's comments. She hasn't liked Mark up until now. She has to reevaluate her feelings and perceptions in light of his comments.

The end of the Sequel brings her to a decision about what to do with the information she now has. She changes the way she feels about Mark. She likes him better now, but decides to proceed with caution because of what she already knows and her own past experiences with him. Her decision sets her up for the next meeting with him. Her attitude and everything she thinks and feels about him will be different than it has been previously. The Sequel has a beginning (reaction), a middle (evaluation) and an end (decision). And that launches the next Scene. That's the important thing you should note about Scenes and Sequels. One leads to the other as surely as a door in your house leads you into another room. At the end of a Sequel the decision the character makes is like taking a step through a doorway, into the next room. In a Scene the resolution at the end is the same. It's like stepping through the doorway into another Scene or a Sequel room. At the end of a Sequel the decision the character makes is like taking a step through a doorway, into the next Scene.

When Bridget looks at her calendar at the end of a harrowing day, she makes the decision that ends this particular Sequel. She sees the scheduled dinner with "smug married couples" and decids to go, even though she isn't looking forward to it.

The resolution of the Scene with the "smug married couples"—Mark's comments—lead to the Sequel where she has to evaluate it all.

Bridget's decision to think of Mark in a different way leads into the next Scene, her assignment to cover the trial where she meets Mark again. Isn't that nifty how they all fit so perfectly together?

In an action-driven story, it isn't unusual to have several Scenes, one after another, before you get to a Sequel, especially the further you get into the story. A character-driven story will usually have more Sequels than an action-driven story, but neither will have more Sequels than Scenes. Your characters have to have something happen before they can react to that something.

Scenes are also usually longer than Sequels. Action keeps the pace steady, at the very least, and hopefully, gradually picks up the speed. Reaction and evaluation—often written as introspection and narrative, and essentially what most Sequels consist of—slow things down. You don't want your story to stay too long, dawdling in the slow lane, or your reader will find something else to do.

PLOTTING WITH STYLE

Those are the very basic things you need to know before you can begin to map out a plot. If you're a Seat-of-the-Pants (SOTP) writer—one who sits down with an idea and a blank page and just writes the story—that may be all you ever need. For those organized Plotters and Planners (P&P)—writers who have to know every aspect of their story before they can begin, this is only a beginning. For those of us who sit down to a blank first page with a certain amount of trepidation unless we have some sort of plan, but can get confused or overwhelmed if we plan *too* much, too far ahead, we need a hybrid of the two styles. We need to be SIB—somewhere in between.

Obviously I don't plan everything up front. I plan some of it, then resort to figuring out the rest as I go. When I get stuck or feel something isn't right, I stop and think through the next part of my story. I suspect this style was part of my problem in understanding plot. Thinking of it as the *story* made me get ahead of myself. Thinking of it as *structure* let me write a portion at a time without worrying about what would be in the next few chapters. As long as the part I was working on had all the elements I needed to make that piece of the story complete, I was on track.

This plot structure is a checklist of sorts. Plotting, using this technique, is making sure all the necessary elements are there in the right amounts and in the most effective order by the time I finish the story. Again, the best way for you to work depends what kind of writer you are.

The kind of writer you are won't decide whether the information from this chapter is useful for you. Your style will probably predict when it will be most helpful to you—before you start (P&P), while you write (SIB), or after you're finished with the first draft and are ready to revise, reorder, and shine your story (SOTP).

Not every story you read or see at the movies will have every element we will discuss, but I can almost guarantee that the ones you remember—the ones you love—will.

Fashions change in what people like to read and write just as they do in everything else. For example, they change in things like Point of View. For many years, most popular fiction was written in third person. In the past few years, we've begun to see more and more first person in every genre. Charles Dickens played God quite handily—with an omniscient point of view—and without apology: ". . . the guard suspected the passengers, the passengers suspected each other and the guard, they all suspected everyone else." But for a long time, seeing things and knowing things that the narrator couldn't possibly know or see was a no-no, almost a sure-fire way to get a rejection from a publisher. J. K. Rowling brought it back into limited style with her Harry Potter series: "Harry Potter slept on, not knowing he was special, not knowing he was famous . . . ."

While Shakespeare used a five-act structure in almost all of his plays, the current fashion in plotting leans toward breaking things into three acts. I divide stories into five parts, and the structure for a plot takes shape. (Though I don't usually think of my parts as acts, we'll use the terminology to keep us on the same page.)

The novel *Pride and Prejudice* wouldn't follow most of the fiction-writing rules you'll find in current writing books. But all five of the story parts I identify below are in that book.

Don't worry about fashions and formulas. There are none, unless you're trying to write a carbon copy of someone else's story—and then it isn't *your* story anyway! This is a plan for structuring your novel, like a blueprint if you were building a house.

THE FIVE MAJOR POINTS OF A FIVE STAR PLOT

Your story as a whole is comprised of five acts:

THE BEGINNING

1ST PIVOTAL POINT

2ND PIVOTAL POINT

3RD PIVOTAL POINT

THE RESOLUTION

When you finish the story, it will earn this star if you have included all of the parts of all of the acts.

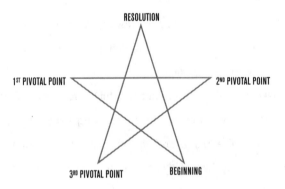

Each of the first four acts (The Beginning and three pivotal points) has five necessary elements to make it complete. So think of each act as a little star hanging on the four points of the larger star, which is your overall story structure.

The Beginning lays the foundation and defines the parts needed to

QUICK TIP: 👈

YOUR REVISION STYLE

SOME WRITERS CAN'T GO ON TO THE NEXT PAGE UNTIL THEY DEEM THE ONE THEY ARE WORKING ON IS PER-FECT. OTHER WRITERS CRASH AND BURN MOMENTUM IF THEY STOP TO CHANGE A THING. STILL OTHERS HAVE TO STOP AND FIND A PROBLEM IF THEY PERCEIVE THAT SOMETHING IS WRONG. THEY CAN'T GO ON UNTIL IT IS FIXED. FIND YOUR STYLE AND DO NOT LET ANYONE CONVINCE YOU THE WAY THEY DO IT IS BETTER. YOUR STORY WILL THANK YOU.

ground your story in either reality or in a world detailed enough to become real to the reader.

The purpose of the Beginning act is to set a tone for the story, set the stage and show the reader the world where our story will take place, intrigue the reader with someone they will care about, and introduce the problem that the character is going to face. This first act (the Beginning) ends with the character acting on a decision.

And the elements—which give us our first small star, in no particular order except for the decision—are:

THE PROBLEM

THE CHARACTER

THE SETTING

THE TONE

THE DECISION

Though thoughts about the decision can come at any time, the act ends and the second act begins when the character actually decides something. Acting on the decision starts the next act.

The Beginning act continues for as few or as many pages as it needs to make the four initial things very clear: the problem, the setting, the tone,

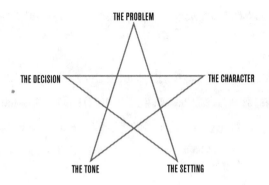

the character. When those things are established, your protagonist can make a decision. For the reader the decision establishes the main character's extrenal goal. When you've planned that much you have the first part of your first star.

If the story is action-driven, you may very well introduce the problem first. A blow-up-the-building prologue, perhaps? If your story is character-driven, odds are you'll want to get the character on the page before or as you introduce the problem.

Perhaps your character has a genuine funny bone and you want to reveal that immediately. Maybe she'll react to the beginnings of the problem, a slap in the face, by laughing. With a beginning like that you could reveal the main character by name, one of the character's main traits—her humor—and a symptom or hint of the problem—the slap—and set the tone, all in one opening sentence.

Setting becomes more important if you are creating a made-up world—such as Krikkit in *The Ultimate Hitchhiker's Guide to the Galaxy* by Douglas Adams—or if you are in a historical time period—35,000 years ago as in *The Clan of the Cave Bear* by Jean M. Auel—or even a real place—say Borneo—that isn't familiar to most readers. But setting is important to define early in

QUICK FIX: 🔧

IF YOU CAN'T FIGURE OUT WHAT HAPPENS NEXT, BRAINSTORM.

MAKE A FAST LIST OF TEN THINGS—WHATEVER POPS INTO YOUR HEAD—OF WHAT *COULD* HAPPEN. TAKE THE THREE MOST LIKELY OR LOGICAL AND BRAINSTORM AGAIN. SEE WHERE EACH OF THOSE IDEAS TAKES YOU.

every story.

You can't have your characters floating about in space and time with no reference that tells the reader where the story is happening. That's especially true if the setting is someplace unique and different from the reality occupied by the reader. He needs a signal to know he'll have to do a mind-shift to comprehend this different world. And you'd be surprised how easily you can establish setting very early in almost any story. The danger lies in getting so detailed that you ruin the launch of your story.

Let's say the problem you plan to introduce is a wrecked car. The heroine will have to have a new one right away or everything she values—her job? her sickly child's visits to the doctor for treatment?—will be threatened. A nice slide on the ice with Molly Mayberry trying to remember if you pump or don't pump the brakes when trying to stop a skid, tells us a lot as she's crashing into the bridge abutment and then caroming off into oncoming traffic.

We have the <u>Problem</u>—so much for *that* car. We have the beginning of a <u>Character</u>—we know her name. Is she screaming hysterically or reacting with cool reason? We know something of her character solely by her reaction and thoughts. Is she one who wears her seatbelt? Those answers give us hints of her character traits.

We have a glimpse of the <u>Setting</u>, too. We know the season—winter because of the ice. She obviously isn't in the tropics. It's probably the "forever now," or the car would be something notably different, like an aircar or a jetpack. As she wonders about pumping the brakes, we know driving on ice isn't something she does every day. The reader will assume she's in a clime more moderate than Alaska, or at least that she's new to the climate she's in. Or she could be new to driving. We have hints.

The Tone is established naturally from the type of story you're telling. But you do have to know and recognize what that tone will be. Is the description of what's happening told in a dramatic tone? A light one? Frivolous? Dark? Your beginning has to be told in the same tone you intend to continue using to tell the whole story.

Your opening scene will probably be told from the main character's perspective. We'll find out her tone, her voice. In the example above, is Molly Mayberry voicing the scene sarcastically in her thoughts? Hysterically? Is the danger to herself uppermost in her mind, or is she worrying about the car? Though a comedic story can have moments of drama—or vice versa—the tone you establish from the beginning must stay consistent throughout the story. And you set it here, from your very first word.

The heroine makes her Decision when she decides she will have to get a new car. The second act starts when she acts on the decision.

That's the breakdown of the first act. Now let's apply it to *Bridget Jones's Diary*.

In the movie, we get a bit of setting, problem, tone, and character in the first line. "It all began on New Year's Day in my thirty-second year of being single." The Setting is partially visual because it's a movie. Bridget (Renée Zellweger) is walking through a heavy snowfall. But we know the time is New Year's Day because she tells us. Her accent is British. (We pick up the accent rather quickly in the print version of the story, too, from the very

British-sounding words she uses.)

The <u>Problem</u> is that she is alone. The fact that she is thirty-two years old and single makes the problem worse. Her mother is trying—as always—to "fix her up." Again, a nod toward the problem. (*Double Duty*: We also get a quick introduction to a second problem, a secondary character and subplot, when Bridget describes her mother as "a strange creature." It's a very insignificant line at the time, but it lays the groundwork for future developments in the subplot.)

From her first line, we know that Bridget is thirty-two years old, and we can deduce that her <u>Character</u> is lonely and concerned about being a spinster. The <u>Tone</u> is quirky. And because it is in Bridget's point of view, we know the character is going to have an interesting—quirky—way of looking at life.

Since this is a character-driven plot, the next five minutes are mostly spent learning about her character and re-emphasizing the problem. She goes without protest to put on the outfit her mother asks her to wear. We know by her description of the outfit—as a "carpet"—that she doesn't especially like it. Why does she put it on? At this point, we don't know if she doesn't stick up for herself, if she doesn't stick up for herself in general because it's her mother, or if she is just easy-going. Our suspicion that she doesn't stick up for herself enough is verified when the fake uncle gropes her butt and asks about her love life—both of which she hates, but does nothing about.

Her father is an ally and sympathetic. She's an optimist. She hopes Mark Darcy (Colin Firth) may be Mr. Right when she sees him from behind. She is verbose without thinking. She isn't very self-disciplined. When Mark Darcy summarizes all the things we've also seen in her character—in the most neg-

QUICK TIP: 👉

PRINT YOUR MANUSCRIPT . . . AS YOU FINISH EACH CHAPTER. PUT IT IN A BINDER OR NOTEBOOK. IF YOU WANT TO LOOK FOR SOMETHING SPECIFIC, USE YOUR WORD PROCESSING *FIND* FEATURE. BUT FOR CHECKING BACK TO SEE WHAT HAPPENED OR EXACTLY WHAT THE CONVERSATION WAS IN A CERTAIN SCENE, YOU'LL FIND THE PRINTED MANUSCRIPT IS EASIER TO READ, BETTER DUPLICATES THE ACT OF READING, AND GIVES YOU SOMETHING TO LEAVE OPEN BESIDE YOU. YOU'LL SAVE YOURSELF A LOT OF SCROLLING.

ative terms possible—Bridget overhears, lifts her chin, smiles, says something inane, and pretends not to have heard. She's learned to put on a pleasant front.

We see her devastation at the insult—and her <u>Decision</u> to change—when she is home alone. Her decision tells us her goal. In the book, we see Bridget's decision—her New Year's resolutions—first, and then her reasons (her <u>motivation</u>) for wanting to change. The same problems, the characterization, the setting, and tone are revealed as we have seen in the movie. We reach the end of the first act and the 1st Pivotal Point, which begins the second act with Bridget taking the first step toward change.

The character of Mark Darcy isn't quite as offensive in the book as he is in the movie, but he makes it clear he isn't interested in having Bridget's phone number. He mostly just avoids her. She returns to her apartment feeling very unattractive.

In *Pride and Prejudice*, Jane Austen's perennial favorite and the book that Helen Fielding loosely based *Bridget Jones's Diary* on, we have a slightly different setup. It was first published in 1813, so it doesn't exactly hold the shape of most current popular fiction. We're introduced to the external goal—the <u>Problem</u>—right away. At least one or two of the five daughters must make a good marriage, or the family may well be destitute when the father dies. His estate is entailed—he is restricted as to who he can leave his property to—and will be inherited by his nephew since he has no male heirs.

We leisurely get to know the primary <u>Characters</u>—Elizabeth, her mother and father, Jane—and several of the secondary ones. The <u>Tone</u> is uniquely Jane Austen's, her time period, her world. And the <u>Setting</u> is especially worth noting.

In the entire first chapter, there is nothing to indicate the weather, whether Mr. and Mrs. Bennet are indoors or out, if they have an audience or are alone. By not mentioning it, we are firmly set in the "forever now." Though it was written nearly two hundred years ago, the "forever now" tells us that it could have been happening around the corner or down the street from most of the readers of the time. Just as a book written in the "forever now" of today—a setting that needs no explanation—would tell the reader the story could be taking place around the corner and down the street in the world they live in now. Setting is sometimes what you don't and shouldn't say.

If the <u>Decision</u> is any one character's, it is the mother's. Mrs. Bennet is intent on her daughters' all being introduced to the new neighbor, Mr. Bingley, because he would make one of them a good match. (After all, she points out frequently, he has 5,000 pounds a year.) Jane and Elizabeth both realize the family fortunes are in their hands and acknowledge they must marry well. But both dream of marrying for love—an external goal. That is also a <u>Decision</u> of sorts, but—because of the restrictions of the time period—destiny isn't fully in their hands.

If act one of your story—the Beginning—includes all these things, it deserves your first small star, with each point representing one of the necessary elements of a good Beginning.

The Beginning leads the character to act on a decision. The plot pivots on that decision, and we're ready for part two, the second act.

The elements needed in the second act, which will lead to the 1st Pivotal Point in the story, are:

CHARACTERIZATION

SECONDS

SETBACKS

SUCCESSES

FAILURE

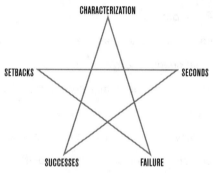

The main character(s) should be introduced by now, with their major traits clear to the reader. In this part of the story, we need to develop her more fully. In a progression of scenes the reader will find out how the character-specific traits cause her to act and react in her day-to-day life. For instance, Bridget doesn't always act in her own best interest. She gets drunk and sings karaoke—badly—at the company party. We'll learn more of the fill-in-the-gap things, such as her current situation. Bridget lives alone, works at a publishing company, and has some very entertaining friends.

Characterization in this part of the book will solidify the audience's initial impressions of the character. This is the introductory phase. She'll face the struggles (conflict) you'll throw at her in a constant barrage. The reader will see how she acts and reacts to those obstacles.

The Seconds in this plot structure refer to secondary plot lines and characters. This is the act where you will introduce and initiate them.

The protagonist will deal mostly with minor obstacles and minor Setbacks in this part of the book, usually related to external goals rather than internal ones, and she'll find some Success—again, mostly in relation to her external goal. She'll take two steps forward and one step back.

By now the character is feeling great about the successes she has had. And in this act, there will probably be more successes than setbacks because the struggles are easy—or so the character thinks. And then she experiences a crashing Failure.

As soon as Bridget makes the decision to change, she succeeds—or so she thinks. With very little effort or action on her part—and a mistake at that, (with her boss catching her in a lie about the phone call from the dead professor—a minor Setback)—she seems to have Daniel's attention (Success). Never mind that avoiding men like Daniel was part of her resolve (Minor Setback in reaching her goal to change since she totally ignores her plan.) We've already established that she doesn't always act wisely. Her overall goal is not to be alone come next New Year's. (Do you see the focus on the external rather than the internal at this point?) He flirts with her skirt (Success). She flirts back, then plays it cool, lecturing herself about finding a nice man (a nod toward her internal goals, more characterization, and a realization on her part that she's experiencing minor Setbacks). Her tally of the number of cigarettes she smokes, the alcoholic units she consumes, and her weight goes up and down (more minor Successes and Setbacks.) He takes her to dinner (Success). They bond talking about Mark Darcy (Success). She worries about her hemlines and how people around her view her. (Her Setbacks and Successes are mostly external, not internal.)

The secondary storyline—her mother's dissatisfaction with her marriage and new boyfriend—is launched (Seconds). We get to know Bridget's friends and all the secondary characters better (Seconds). She and Daniel take a mini-break. "Oh joy! No longer a tragic spinster . . . A mini-break means true love" (Success). "Daniel? Do you love me?" He doesn't exactly answer (Setback). He zips out and leaves her to face the Tarts and Vicars party alone (Setback). Bridget finds him with another woman. (Failure). You've reached the 1st Pivotal Point.

In *Pride and Prejudice*, Jane makes headway in the marriage stakes. The new neighbor, Mr. Bingley, is very much taken with her and she with him (Success). There are a couple of flies in the ointment though: his sisters and his friend (Setback). And it doesn't help that they consider her family far beneath Mr. Bingley on the societal scale (Setback). Jane falls ill while visiting Mr. Bingley's sister (Success for Mrs. Bennet). Elizabeth goes to care for her sister and is subjected to Miss Bingley's snobbery (Setback).

Elizabeth is not doing as well in the marriage stakes. Mr Bingley's friend, Mr. Darcy, doesn't even find her "tolerable" enough to dance with (Setback). After overhearing that conversation, she forms a very prejudiced opinion of the conceited Mr. Darcy.

She does attract the attention of a new officer in town, Mr. Wickham (Success), but he doesn't have the means to support a wife and needs to find someone himself who can bring financial backing to a marriage (Setback). They bond over their shared dislike of Mr. Darcy (Seconds).

Mr. Collins, the male cousin who will inherit the Bennet estate, is determined to find a wife and asks Elizabeth to marry him (Seconds and Success). She finds him intolerable (Setback). We get to know all of the family better (Characterization and Seconds) and find that the mother and younger sisters do not always exhibit the most proper behavior (Seconds and Setback).

After an especially obnoxious display on the part of the Bennet family, the Bingley party departs for London, leaving behind a very disappointed Jane. The hopes of any of the daughters forming a "good match" with Mr. Bingley turn to dust (Failure).

If this act has shown your character acting and reacting with the character traits you have given her, if it has introduced your secondary story lines and characters, if you've shown your character finding some success and experiencing some setbacks, followed by a major failure, your second act is complete. You've reached your 1st Pivotal Point and earned another star.

The failure at the end of the second act leads the character to reevaluate and renew her resolve to reach her goal. The plot pivots to act three, (and takes you to the 2nd Pivotal Point.) Act three of your story will need:

RENEWAL

OBSTACLES

SUCCESSES

GROWTH

REAL RISK

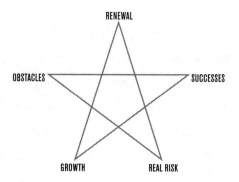

Whatever the character's goal, after her Failure realizes that reaching it is not going to be as easy as she thought it would be.

It's human nature to resist change. We all do it, especially if the change is difficult. Up until now—during the second part of your story—that is what the character has been doing. She's been resisting real change by making virtually effortless moves, taking the easy way out, if you will.

She Renews her commitment to the goal, even though she realizes it is going to be tough. She begins to make the less obvious changes she needs to make. She begins working internally instead of just superficially. The Obstacles get larger. Her struggles require greater effort. But her Successes are bigger, too. The reader starts to see real Growth and change in the character. And the character becomes more aware of how she's changing. She begins to feel a sense of satisfaction that she is making them. Then something happens to make the character put her goal at *risk*.

After Bridget throws her well-deserved pity party, we see her Renewal when she tells her diary, "I have two choices. I can give up and accept permanent state of spinsterhood and eventual eating by dogs . . . or Not. And this time, I choose Not."

Daniel points her in the right direction for internal change when he tells her his new American fiancée has "confidence." Bridget throws out all her self-help books geared toward supplying a man with what he wants and replaces them with books about how to get what *she* wants. Her <u>Obstacles</u> get bigger as she looks for a new job, but her successes do, too. She lands a very different but potentially great job, and we see <u>Growth</u> as she finally gets to confidently tell Daniel she'd rather "wipe Saddam Hussein's ass" than work for him.

Her first effort at her new job is less than stellar—demoralizing in fact. A dinner with "smug married couples" (Obstacle), bottoms out the demoralizing day. But Mark Darcy bolsters her confidence by telling her he likes her just the way she is (Success).

Her next job assignment turns out much better. "Oh Joy! I am broadcasting genius." This time she celebrates something she did, her own achievement, something deeper than what's on the surface. (Growth again and *Double Duty*: Success with Mark).

She is celebrating her <u>Success</u> with her friends and with a newly appealing Mark Darcy—since he contributed greatly to her "broadcasting genius" success—when Daniel turns up again.

Mark and Daniel fight—over her (Big-time Success)! Yet when it comes right down to it, based on what she's learned (Growth), she turns them both away, putting her goal of not being alone at risk (Real risk). She tells Daniel she is still looking for something more extraordinary than he offers.

An amazingly well-told story—explaining its popularity for almost 200 years—*Pride and Prejudice* is also a product of its time. The elements are tricky to compare to current popular fiction because the overall goals are broad, not those of individual characters, and the societal restrictions made it difficult for the characters—especially women—to make decisions that would make a real difference in their lives. Most of the changes that take place are in attitude and outlook. Success and Growth in this story are often measured by how the characters deal with life as it was, not in how they substantially changed their lives, though that was a part of it.

At the 1st Pivotal Point, Jane Bennet, who always assumes the best of everyone, goes to London in hopes of running into Mr. Bingley again. (Renewal) She is treated to the snobbery that Elizabeth first experienced from Mr. Bingley's sisters (Obstacle). She admits that perhaps not everyone is as kind and well-wishing as she gives them credit for being (Growth). She doesn't see Mr. Bingley (Obstacle).

Elizabeth is strong-willed and jumps to conclusions on very short acquaintance. Her character growth relies on learning to live with the consequences of her prejudices and on not forming her opinions so quickly. She admits to loving few and liking even fewer. "The more I see of the world, the more am I dissatisfied with it," she says, "and everyday confirms my belief of the inconsistency of all human characters, and of the little dependence that can be placed on the appearance of either merit or sense."

She becomes friendlier with Mr. Wickham (Renewal), though she knows a relationship with him holds few possibilities because of their fortunes—or lack of them (Obstacle). By listening to his prejudices, she makes some judgments that will have a negative impact on her family (Obstacle). When her best friend Charlotte marries Mr. Collins, the man she turned down, Elizabeth is, at first, appalled on her friend's behalf. Then she grows more tolerant of the choices others make (Growth). Except in the case of Mr. Darcy.

She goes to visit Mr. Collins and Charlotte and finds herself often in close proximity to Mr. Darcy. She verbally spars with him at every opportunity—and usually wins (Success). She finds from his companion, Colonel Fitzwilliams, that Mr. Darcy was instrumental in separating Jane from Mr. Bingley. Her prejudice against Mr. Darcy grows by a *huge* bound.

Mr. Darcy—stunningly—proposes to her (Success!) by naming all the reasons he should not want a marriage with her: her family and her low social status (Setback). He tells her he likes her against his will, his reason, and even against his character. Mr. Darcy is very wealthy, much too high in society to consider marrying someone as lowly as she is and still think of it as a "good" marriage for himself. He asks her to marry him because he loves her, and risks *his* respectability.

She *should* be flattered (Success). But she dreams of marrying for love, and all he has done is insult her and her family. She makes it clear that she doesn't respect him.

Elizabeth turns him down (Real Risk) putting the goal of marrying well to secure her family's future security in jeopardy. As Mr. Collins warned her, there are few chances she will get more proposals of marriage and none that she will get a better one than from Mr. Darcy.

Your story gets another gold star if you can confirm that all of these elements are included in this part of your story:

RENEWAL

OBSTACLES

SUCCESSES

GROWTH

REAL RISK

With that Real Risk, your plot reaches the 2nd Pivotal point and act four begins.

From the protagonist's point of view, act four leading to the 3rd and final Pivotal Point is mainly about the internal changes she has to make. But it is also where you resolve subplots and problems that have to do with secondary characters. Act four of your story should include (in no particular order):

SECONDS

CHANGE

REALITY CHECK

BLACK MOMENT

ULTIMATE RISK

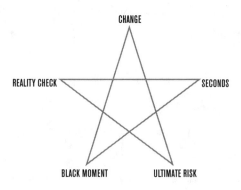

The items needed to have a satisfactory fourth act in a story truly don't need to happen in any specific order.

This is the point in the story where you tie up loose ends. Secondary plots—<u>Seconds</u>—are resolved. Secondary characters resolve any outstand-

QUICK TIP:

THE BEGINNING OF THE END

DON'T BE SURPRISED IF YOUR STORY PACE PICKS UP AT THE 3RD PIVOTAL POINT. MOST OF THE DETAILS YOU NEEDED TO MAKE THE CHARACTERS WELL-ROUNDED, OR TO ADD SPICE, ATMOSPHERE, OR COLOR, OR TO EXPLAIN WHAT IS GOING ON ARE IN PLACE NOW. DON'T FEEL OBLIGED TO ADD DETAILS THAT—AT THIS POINT—JUST SEEM REDUNDANT. LET YOUR PLOT CARRY YOU ALONG TO A FAST-PACED AND SATISFYING CONCLUSION.

ing conflicts. Any questions remaining must be answered. In order for the character to <u>Change</u>, core beliefs must be challenged. She must finally realize the error of her ways. Then she must take the steps necessary to make the change. A <u>Reality Check</u> is anything that tests the character's resolve to make the change. An obstacle that would have defeated her previously is now determinedly disregarded. The character is now willing to take the <u>Ultimate Risk</u> of failure. After the character takes the <u>Ultimate Risk</u>, the outcome is often out of her hands. The risk leads to crisis—the <u>Black Moment</u>, which occurs when it seems that the protagonist has, indeed, lost everything, including hope of reaching her goal (some call this the climax). The <u>Black Moment</u> describes it perfectly for me in that it is the dark before the dawn.

In some stories the character's change results in the <u>Black Moment</u>, and induces the character to take the <u>Ultimate Risk</u>. In others, the <u>Black Moment</u> forces the change. In action-driven plots, character change is often so subtle that you miss it unless you're intent on looking for it. (Think *Speed* again.) Sometimes the character takes the <u>Ultimate Risk</u> and then comes face-to-face with the <u>Black Moment</u>.

Again, the elements needed in Act Four do not have to happen in any

QUICK TIP: 👉

KEEP A LIST . . .

OF SECONDARY CHARACTERS OR PLOT LINES OR ANYTHING THAT NEEDS TO BE ADDRESSED AGAIN. MAKE IT AS YOU WRITE, ADDING TO IT AS ANY ITEM APPEARS THAT WILL HAVE TO BE ADDRESSED LATER. REFER BACK TO IT AND CROSS OFF EACH ITEM AS IT IS COVERED. YOU'LL GET TO THE END WITHOUT LEAVING ANY QUESTIONS UNANSWERED OR YOUR READERS DANGLING.

particular order; just so all the pieces are there.

Bridget shows Change at the moment the plot pivots again. Does she want just any man or does she want a "nice" man as she first stated in her resolutions? She chooses being alone over Daniel Cleaver.

When she goes home for Christmas, her mother appears and her parents reunite (Seconds). The Change continues when she discovers that she has been wrong about Mark Darcy. Her decision to turn him away was based on inaccurate information. She determinedly sets out to correct the problem.

Bridget's Reality Check comes when she arrives at Mark's party for his parents' anniversary. She first sees Mark in a crowd. She plunges ahead. Mark isn't exactly receptive or encouraging. She plunges ahead anyway. Natasha interrupts them. Bridget plunges ahead again. She takes the Ultimate Risk and gets him alone to have her say. They are interrupted. Mark goes back to the party without reacting.

Bridget's Black Moment comes when she discovers Mark is leaving the country and becoming engaged to Natasha. Still true to her verbally incontinent self, she plunges ahead, she protests loudly, extending her Ultimate Risk. She returns home, defeated, feeling all is lost.

Elizabeth, in *Pride and Prejudice*, begins to <u>Change</u> almost as soon as she rejects Mr. Darcy. She receives his letter, telling her the irrefutable facts of his relationship with Mr. Wickham. She sees her family and situation from his point of view. A visit to the lake country with her aunt and uncle cements the <u>Change</u>. She visits his estate and hears about his real character from his housekeeper. She meets him again and he goes out of his way to be gentlemanly and cordial to her and her aunt and uncle—even though they are also socially inferior to him. (Mr. Darcy is changing, too, but we've had most of the focus on Elizabeth so we'll stay there.) Mr. Darcy invites them to his home and introduces her to his sister.

Elizabeth's <u>Change</u> is complete when Lydia, her youngest sister, runs off with Mr. Wickham. She realizes her mistaken assumptions have contributed to her problems and have, in fact, helped make what has happened possible. She knows she and her whole family will have to deal with the consequences of her mistakes.

On hearing the news about Lydia's behavior, Mr. Darcy seemingly turns his back on her.

Elizabeth hits her <u>Black</u> <u>Moment</u> when she and Jane console each other with the knowledge that Lydia's blemish on the family's reputation means they have little hope of marrying at all, let alone of marrying well or for love.

Lydia is found, and Mr. Wickham is forced to marry her (Seconds). Mr. Bingley returns and proposes marriage to Jane (Seconds).

Elizabeth's <u>Reality</u> <u>Check</u> begins when she finds that Mr. Darcy is the one who secretly brought about a resolution to the situation with Lydia and Mr. Wickham. When he comes to visit with Mr. Bingley, her mother persists in insulting him. The <u>Reality</u> <u>Check</u> continues when Mr. Darcy's aunt comes to call to warn Elizabeth not to marry Mr. Darcy. After all of that, does she still dare hope that he cares?

She fears she will never know unless she takes the Ultimate Risk. She apologizes and offers her thanks to Mr. Darcy for his part in solving the problem with Lydia and Mr. Wickham. She knows that she is giving him the opening he needs to declare himself, if he is still interested. If he doesn't take it, she'll know hope is gone.

And your plot has reached at the 3rd pivotal point, of the Ultimate Risk, and the final act begins.

THE RESOLUTION

There is only one thing left at this point. Either the character will get what she wants or she will fail. The scene (or scenes) that shows whether your protagonist walks away with the prize is the sum total of the resolution.

In both Bridget and Elizabeth's cases, they succeed.

In *Bridget Jones's Diary*, Mark Darcy returns to England to get the kiss he forgot to get before he left. In *Pride and Prejudice*, Mr. Darcy asks Elizabeth if her feelings have changed. She admits they have. And Elizabeth and Bridget both achieve their ultimate goal (Resolution).

Whether your character succeeds or fails, you have succeeded in building a stellar plot if you have included all of the things we've discussed. Double-check your plot with the Five Star Plot Checklist (Appendix E) or use the 10 Step Plot Planner (Appendix D) to map yours out.

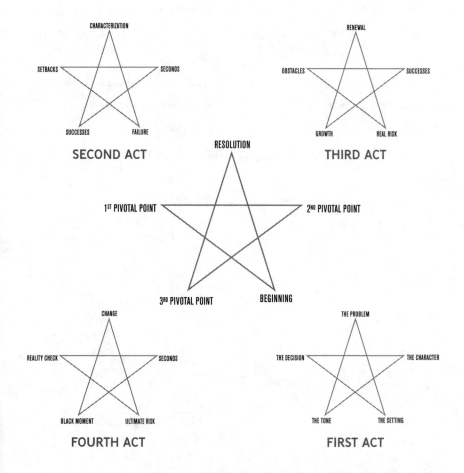

SECOND ACT

THIRD ACT

FOURTH ACT

FIRST ACT

NOTE:

A REALITY CHECK FOR AUTHORS. REMEMBER THE SCENE WHERE THE PUBLISHING COMPANY IS "LAUNCHING" A BOOK? SEVERAL FAMOUS AUTHORS MAKE AN APPEARANCE, INCLUDING SALMAN RUSHDIE. HE PLAYS ALONG WITH AN INSIDE JOKE, ESPECIALLY MEANT FOR AUTHORS I WOULD BET. TWICE, SOMEONE ASKS HIM WHERE THE BATHROOM IS.

AT AN AUTHOR'S FIRST BOOK-SIGNING, HE HOPES FOR—AND DESERVES—A LITTLE AWE AND ADMIRATION . . . ONLY TO DISCOVER THAT NO ONE, NO MATTER HOW MIGHTY, GETS BY WITHOUT AT LEAST ONE PERSON COMING UP TO ASK—NOT FOR AN AUTOGRAPH—BUT FOR DIRECTIONS TO THE BATHROOM.

PLAN ON IT! IT'S PART OF THE PLOT TO KEEP AUTHORS FIRMLY GROUNDED IN REALITY.

Chapter Ten

Putting It All Together . . . and Other Tricks of the Trade

ASSIGNMENT: *JAWS*

Most of us have a junk drawer. The junk drawer is where you stash the stuff you aren't sure what else to do with. It's the place you look when don't know where else to look for—or can't find—that small roll of fishing line you didn't want to throw away because you knew it would come in handy someday.

Consider this chapter the junk drawer. I'm sticking bits and pieces I've learned from watching various movies here. They're things that deserve some mention because they may help you at some point, but they don't merit a whole chapter. We're also going to look at examples of everything we've

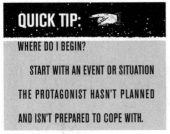

QUICK TIP:

WHERE DO I BEGIN?

START WITH AN EVENT OR SITUATION
THE PROTAGONIST HASN'T PLANNED
AND ISN'T PREPARED TO COPE WITH.

discussed using the movie *Jaws*.

Besides having great illustrations of the things we've studied, the structure of *Jaws* is action-driven versus the character-driven story we considered in *Bridget Jones's Diary*. You might find it useful to see how they are different and yet the same. *Jaws* is also based on a book by the same name, so it gives us ample opportunity to compare the written version with the movie. And despite its age, the movie doesn't seem to get dated.

I've added a few time markers from the DVD (Anniversary Collector's Edition) so you can easily find some things you may want to see again.

BEGINNINGS

As the song from *The Sound Of Music* goes, the very beginning is a very good place to start. When you first begin a story, you don't always know exactly where the *start* is. For the most part, you can't study movies and learn much about that because movies do a lot of things that don't work very well in books. *Jaws* is an exception. It sticks very closely to the way Peter Benchley opened his novel.

You'll hear in writing workshops that you should "start with the action in progress." When I began my first book, I thought that meant action, as in movement. I started that story with ten pages of what I thought was *action* because my character was driving somewhere. (My protagonist was also thinking about what, in her life, had led her on this trip, so I assumed I was doing characterization as well.) I found out later that *action* in the phrase "action in progress" is fictional shorthand for Conflict and Struggle. "Start with the action in progress" isn't my favorite way to describe a good beginning.

Another thing you'll hear is that you should "start on the day that is different." Well, in that first attempt, driving for ten pages was a day that was different for my heroine. She was running away from something and that wasn't her normal day. The big mistake I made was thinking I had to tell the reader who she was before I could actually get on with the story. Wrong!

Had I started with the accident that happened about two-thirds through my first chapter, I would have been fine. That was something she hadn't planned. And that's how I like to say you should start a book. Start with something the hero or heroine hasn't planned and isn't prepared to face.

Action-driven plots often start by introducing the problem first. *Jaws* starts with a scene that compares with the prologue of many books. We are first introduced to the <u>Problem</u> the main character, Chief Brody (Roy Scheider) is going to face: a shark! The shark chows down on a woman skinny-dipping in the middle of the night. (Benchley didn't call it a prologue. He called it Chapter One. But that's one of those decisions you—the God of your made-up world—get to make. It isn't a right or wrong choice unless someone spending money to buy your story—an editor—tells you it is.)

We immediately meet the <u>Character</u> who is going to have to resolve that <u>Problem</u>. We don't get to know Brody intimately in some long, drawn-out, getting-to-know-you sequence of scenes. We get to know who he is—his characteristics, his idiosyncrasies—bit by bit, learning something new about him via a line of dialogue here, an action or reaction there. For instance, he's a caring father. (We see the way he deals with his kids as he leaves for work.) He's overly confident he can handle his job. (He compares it to working in the city as he leaves for work.) We discover he's an outsider and new to his job when he questions the way they "do things here," after the body is discovered on the beach—and not quite so confident with *this* situation. Though some of the characters in the movie differ extensively from the characters in the book, the way we get to know Chief Brody is the same in both the book and the movie. We get acquainted with him scene by scene, a detail here and a detail there. By the time we're a quarter of the way into the story, Chief Brody's character is well established.

The thing you need to remember about book beginnings is that the second we start learning about the characters, the story should also be unfolding. And vice versa. As the story unfolds, we should learn more about the characters.

Brody is a cop. The first two lines of dialogue between him and his wife tell us they are new in town. (First Character trait: he doesn't belong. He's a fish out of water—excuse the pun.) Though the Setting has been partially identified in the prologue—we know he's near an ocean—we get the name of the place and the fact that it is an island when he drives past the sign that reads "Amity Island Welcomes You." The Tone is dramatic. He takes his new responsibilities (2nd Character trait) seriously, but he isn't concerned that he won't be able to handle the job. "Chief, be careful," his wife (Lorraine Gary) tells him, also telling us his title. "In this town?" he mocks. Then he learns the Problem. He immediately decides to close the beaches to protect his citizens. With that Decision, the story is launched. (Benchley and his co-screenwriter, Carl Gottlieb, get their first plotting star.)

Brody's External Goal is established for us with his decision: He wants to get rid of the shark. Why? To protect his town. Why? So he and his family can belong. We know the surface edge of his <u>Motivation</u>.

His <u>Internal</u> <u>Goal</u>? To be capable of defeating this foe. (<u>Inferiority</u> <u>Complex</u>: He feels very confident and capable of being the Chief of Police in this small town—until it involves water and sharks and things he has no experience with and has no desire to experience.) The first artichoke petal is peeled away.

The <u>Premise</u>? Personal responsibility leads to success. (Success, in this instance, is defined as being capable of getting rid of/killing the shark.)

The <u>Theme</u> is Belonging. Brody doesn't belong here. The shark doesn't belong here. Brody will never belong if he can't deliver on his responsibility to protect the town.

IST PIVOTAL POINT

When Brody decides to close the beaches, the story makes its first pivot. He also establishes a <u>Short-term</u> and <u>Mid-term</u> <u>Goal</u> right then. (Short-term: to get some young boys who are practicing diving out of the water. Mid-term: to actually close the beaches.) Then we learn that if he closes the beaches, he is going to hurt the town's economy (<u>Conflict</u>: Does he protect the town from the shark? Or from horrible economic conditions?) It isn't his choice, (Setback) he quickly finds out. "Under whose authority?" a merchant asks, and then tells him, "It takes a Civic Ordinance or a resolution by the Board of Selectmen." (Brody may not "be capable" of reaching his <u>External</u> <u>Goal</u>. It might not be in his power. *Double Duty*: <u>Reader</u> <u>Identification</u>—we all know the frustrated feeling of being helpless.)

We're learning more about Brody. (We're in the <u>Introductory</u> <u>Stage</u> of <u>Characterization</u>. The <u>Establishment</u> <u>Stage</u> happens during the author's planning phase.) He's a responsible and caring family man, as well as a responsible and caring Chief. We discover that he took the job here because "One man can make a difference . . ." He didn't feel that way about being a cop in New York. He doesn't like water (<u>Internal</u> <u>Goal</u>: He, personally, does not feel capable of reaching his external goal. How can he kill a shark if he is afraid to go in the water?) Though he's dealt with the kinds of crime they have in the city, things like bodies on beaches are out of his league. "What do they usually do? Wash up or float?" (<u>Message</u> <u>to</u> <u>the</u> <u>Audience</u> that Brody really may not be capable of doing his job. We're peeling away more artichoke petals.)

Is Brody <u>heroic</u>? He passes the test, either way you ask the question. He's mostly a common man in an uncommon situation in that he's an everyday, ordinary small town Chief of Police. Not many of those face a shark as public enemy number one. But he's also an uncommon man in a common situation in that he's the new guy in town, the outsider, a big-city guy still feeling his way around a small town with its power struggles and political games.

With the introduction of Mayor Vaughan (<u>Secondary</u> character played by Murray Hamilton) and the town's economy, a <u>Secondary</u> story line commences. We see street banners heralding the upcoming 4th of July celebration in town. (*Double Duty*: the banner <u>Foreshadows</u> an important event and tells us there is a deadline, a <u>Time</u> <u>Bomb</u> The banner is also a good example of sneaky ways of getting details into your story without having characters say inane things.) The economy hinges on a successful holiday weekend. Mayor Vaughan tells Brody he can close the beaches for twenty-four hours (*Double Duty*: Brody reaches a mid-term <u>Goal</u> and experiences a small Success).

Brody has painted "Beach Closed" signs, closed the beaches for twenty-four hours, called an oceanographer for expert help, and studied books on sharks. As Brody is turning pages and looking at pictures in one book, we briefly glimpse a picture of a shark with an oxygen tank in his mouth. We've set in motion the first part of the Rule of Three, which will help make the unbelievable believable (*Double Duty*: Foreshadowing the end). He hasn't done anything directly related to getting rid of the shark. He hasn't done anything proactive about his antagonist at all.

Then a boy is killed.

While the people around him are running into the water to pull people out, Brody stands on the shore and yells for them to get out (Show-don't-tell characterization and *Double Duty*: With his automatic reaction, his fear of water—(a Character Trait) is reinforced. The question of his capabilities in this situation—(his Internal Goal)—is reinforced.)

From this point on, any characterization for Brody is in the proving stage. He just has to remain true to the character that we have discovered him to be.

The boy's mother offers a reward for the shark. The town fills with fishermen and is in chaos (*Double Duty*: Obstacle and Brody's outsider status is reinforced when he tells his deputy to "talk to them. You at least know their names.")

And then Hooper (Richard Dreyfuss), the oceanographer, arrives. He checks the first victim and immediately intensifies Brody's feelings of inadequacy. "Didn't you get on a boat and check it out?" "Didn't you notify the Coast Guard?"

A big shark is caught by some of the fishermen. The town is celebrating. Brody is feeling really good (<u>Success</u>–though *too* easy and with little effort on his part).

Mayor Vaughan is practically crowing with glee. Hooper is warning Brody that this might not be *their* shark. (Study a great example of <u>Body</u> <u>Language</u> at Time Marker 35:18 in

QUICK FIX: ⚒

IF YOUR STORY IS STUCK . . .

READ YOUR MANUSCRIPT FROM THE BEGINNING TO . . . WHEREVER YOU ARE. EVEN IF IT TAKES SEVERAL HOURS. THAT WILL ALMOST ALWAYS GET YOU GOING AGAIN, AND IT BEATS WASTING HOURS STARING AT YOUR MONITOR.

Chapter 9 on the DVD. With facial expressions, Scheider tells us a lot. Brody doesn't *want* to believe what Hooper is saying. He wants to celebrate with everyone else. Hooper mentions the bite radius. Brody doesn't know anything about sharks or bite radius, but as a big-city cop, he is accustomed to working with solid, scientific evidence. This sounds like scientific evidence. His smile wavers, then slowly disintegrates. He no longer meets Hooper's eyes. He looks down, sideways, anywhere but at Hooper, trying to ignore the facts.)

The little boy's mother walks up and slaps Chief Brody in the face. "You knew," she says and accuses him of letting her son die. As she walks away, Mayor Vaughan tells Brody, "I'm sorry, Martin. She's wrong."

"No. She's not," he replies. Brody knows he has failed. Utterly and unequivocally. He's responsible. He didn't personally *do* anything. He hasn't protected his town (<u>Failure</u>).

2ND PIVOTAL POINT

The <u>Conflict</u> with the boy's mother renews Brody's determination (<u>Renewal</u>). He learns more about his adversary from Hooper (<u>Growth</u>).

The screenwriters treat the shark like another character, an antagonist. They <u>Characterize</u> him with pieces of knowledge we learn from Brody's books, from Hooper and various sources, and also by the shark's actions and reactions. Though we've all seen the same approach attempted by others, few are as successful. Most of the time when this is tried, the information comes in soliloquies that make you feel is if you've just landed in a classroom lecture. Benchley and Gottlieb managed to give the shark character traits in context—as an answer to a random question, as opposed to a question and answer session that feels like scientific research; or as a fact that comes through as someone relates a personal experience. For example: Mrs. Brody asks about Hooper's love of sharks. He tells her how he got interested in them and fits in some useful information, too. (He also leaves a <u>Foreshadowing Marker</u> when he talks about a shark eating his boat.)

Hooper and Brody go to "open up" the shark caught earlier in the day. They want to see, once and for all, if it is their shark. Mrs. Brody questions whether or not they can do that. "I can do anything," Brody replies, "I'm the Chief." (*Double duty*: <u>Obstacle</u>—someone may have a problem with it. <u>Growth</u>: He's putting himself in position to *be* more capable.) They confirm that it is not their shark. (*Double Duty*: <u>Success</u> and <u>Setback</u>—they are certain but it also means that they still have a problem.)

QUICK TIP:

IF YOUR WRITING TIME IS LIMITED . . .

RETYPE IN THE LAST PAGE-AND-A-HALF YOU WROTE IN YOUR LAST SESSION. (A PARAGRAPH OR TWO MAY DO, DEPENDING ON HOW LONG IT HAS BEEN SINCE YOU WORKED.) DO NOT REVISE, JUST TYPE AND READ. THAT WILL GET YOUR MOMENTUM BACK SO THAT YOU WON'T WASTE TIME TRYING TO GET BACK INTO THE STORY.

Brody goes out on the water with Hooper (<u>Growth</u>: he's becoming more capable).

The <u>stakes continually go up</u>. The first victim of the shark was an outsider, a summer tourist. The second, the little boy, is a local. The economy is threatened. A $3,000 reward is up for grabs. The mayor tells Brody to do whatever he needs to do, but beaches will *not* be closed on the 4th (<u>Obstacle</u>).

The 4th of July comes. The beaches are packed. Brody has put on extra help, boats patrolling the water, helicopters; he has people patrolling the beach. He convinces his son to take his boat to the "pond." (<u>Success</u>.)

The <u>Struggles</u> get more <u>personal</u>. Brody's son has a boat. He does not want his son even sitting in the boat tied to a dock. He protects his son by sending him to the pond instead. The shark attacks in the pond. Brody's attempts to close the beaches—taking away the shark's food source—to hire extra help, to bring in an expert—everything he has tried—are all worthless. Up to now, at least subconsciously, he's been able to blame his failure on red tape, the mayor, a shark that is going against its nature in that it doesn't belong where it is. The dead boy's mother put it all on him: he has to accept personal responsibility and take <u>personal</u> action.

At the hospital, he tells his wife to take their son home. "Home to New York?" she asks. "No here, home." He is *going* to belong! He forces the mayor to sign a voucher authorizing him to go after the shark. (<u>Real</u> <u>Risk</u>: He is ready to put himself and his job on the line.)

3RD PIVOTAL POINT

Brody hires Quint (Robert Shaw) to lead the hunt for the shark. We see a change in Brody's determination. He's taking charge. (<u>Character</u> <u>Change</u>: "It's my party. My charter," he tells Quint.)

Unfortunately, Brody's still the odd man out. Though Quint and Hooper resent each other practically on sight, they both know what they are doing (<u>Theme</u>: they belong). Quint begins to teach Brody how to tie nautical knots, and Hooper lectures the Chief when he pulls the wrong knot, letting an air tank fall. Hooper explains how explosive compressed air is (the <u>Rule of Three</u>, Point #2). And the next time the air tanks are jostled, Brody carefully secures them.

> **QUICK TIP:**
>
> **FINDING YOUR STYLE**
>
> FIND YOUR OWN TECHNIQUES, GIMMICKS, AND TRICKS TO CONVEY THINGS TO READERS. AS LONG YOU ARE CONSISTENT THROUGHOUT YOUR STORY, READERS WILL GET YOUR MESSAGE AND YOU WILL DEVELOP YOUR OWN UNIQUE STYLE.

Though the story is mostly about Brody's struggles, Quint and Hooper are definitely primary characters in the movie. Both have stories of their own. <u>Conflict</u> between Quint and Hooper dominates the next several scenes as they begin the hunt for the Great White shark (advances the <u>Secondary</u> storyline).

Hooper is a well-educated, poor little rich kid following his passion. Quint is a working-class hero following his obsession. We all identify with Hooper when he tells Quint, "Hey, I don't need this working-class hero crap" when they first meet. (We've all been judged without being given a chance: <u>Reader</u> <u>Identification/Universal</u> <u>Language</u>). But we've also had the luxury of getting to know Hooper a bit. We find him charming, even though he is arrogant. Remember, when he first came to Brody's house, he walked in without waiting for an invitation, then asked "what's for dinner" and helped himself to the meal Brody hadn't eaten. He also tried to stop Brody from pouring the wine he'd brought—"Hey, you should let that breathe . . . ." Arrogance! (Characterization.)

We also identify quickly with Quint when he tells Hooper, "(It) proves that you wealthy college boys don't have the education to admit when you are wrong." (We've all been there with some snot-nosed know-it-all who won't admit he's wrong: Reader Identification/Universal Language.)

SECONDARY CHARACTERS

In the book and the movie, we get to know the major characters a piece at a time. Benchley uses an interesting technique in introducing us to secondary characters in his book. (Quint was a secondary in the book.) At first appearance, Benchley gives each one several pages of profile. We learn most of anything we need to know about them. The method he uses to introduce them distinguishes them *as* secondary characters.

Whether a major character or a secondary one, few characters are more memorable than Quint is in this movie. From the moment he introduces himself in the movie—by screeching his fingernails down a blackboard—he grates on everyone's nerves. (Isn't *that* a terrific bit of Show-Don't-Tell Characterization? And don't think that was just visual, only effective in a movie. Did you just get a chill when reading the words "screeching his fingernails down a blackboard"? Remember the five senses. You have to convey every one of them with words, and you can do it by picking your words carefully.)

Grating and annoying is the way we see Quint throughout most of the story. Quint changes every perception we have about him with a sparse bit of dialogue and his spare, matter-of-fact telling of his experiences as a survivor of the *U.S.S. Indianapolis*. We suddenly know everything we need to know about how Quint has become the man he is. Knowing what made him the obsessed man he is (<u>motivation</u>) transforms him into a truly sympathetic character.

In the book, Quint is also grating and irritating, but we are never given a reason for it. I don't know of a more powerful example of how understanding a character's <u>motivation</u> can substantially affect <u>reader</u> <u>identification</u>. Making clear *why* a character acts the way he does (his history) can dramatically change how the audience reacts to (and remembers) your story. Thus the audience cares deeply when the shark gets Quint in the movie. And it feels inevitable—the smashed radio, pushing the motor until it gives out—as if he, Quint, were destined to end this way. His death in the book, though sad, barely takes our focus from the fight with the shark.

TRANSITIONS

Weak transitions are one of the first and most obvious mistakes you see in the work of a fledgling writer—or a fledgling moviemaker.

Good transitions mean that one thing leads logically to another, and another, and another. Something can't come from nothing. Whether we're talking about scenes or a conversation or a single line of dialogue, something has to inspire or lead into it.

Good transitions are hard to write. Not having one is on my top three list of things that slow me down and rob me of getting down the seven pages I intend to write each day. I know what is supposed to happen next. I know where the story is going. But I can't find a way into the scene or important conversation so I stumble around, only to find that the day has gone and I

QUICK FIX:

IF THE PACE FEELS WRONG . . .

CHECK SENTENCE STRUCTURE. LONG SENTENCES WITH LOTS OF QUALIFIERS AND DESCRIPTION AND MODIFIERS ARE THOUGHT-PROVOKING, BUT SLOW THE READER DOWN. (THAT'S NOT NECESSARILY A BAD THING.) SHORT, SPARSE SENTENCES READ QUICKLY.

IF YOUR USUAL STYLE CONSISTS OF LONGER AND MORE COMPLEX SENTENCES, SHORT SENTENCES WILL CHANGE THE PACE. IF YOUR USUAL STYLE IS SHORT AND DIRECT, A LENGTHY, COMPLEX, COMPOUND SENTENCE CAN MAKE THE READER BREATHLESS. REMEMBER THAT A PERIOD SIGNALS A BREAK FOR A SHORT BREATH, EVEN IF THE READER IS NOT READING ALOUD. MAKE THE READER RUSH TO THE END OF A SENTENCE TO CATCH HIS BREATH WITH LONG SENTENCES. OR MAKE THEM PANT WITH SHORT ONES. VARYING SENTENCE STRUCTURE WORKS MAGIC, TOO.

have two pages to show for it.

A good transition often comes from a tiny, telling <u>detail</u> that goes almost unnoticed. When the three fishermen first encounter their prey—they get a hit on their fishing line—a physical skirmish ensues. Brody falls. Quint notices blood when things calm down and points Brody toward the first-aid kit.

As night falls (in my favorite scene of the movie, Chapter 15 on the DVD), Quint sees Brody checking his wound. Quint assures Brody that it will be okay. That comment transitions Hooper and Quint into a conversation about their scars.

Whether Brody's wound was a gift from the writers' subconscious or whether it came from working backward, it brought about a transition that would have been tough to make without it. What else would have gotten those two, Hooper and Quint, talking about and comparing their wounds, especially since they aren't all that friendly to begin with?

The conversation starts as a competition, but it brings about a resolution to the <u>Secondary</u> conflict going on between the Hooper and Quint. In body language you see them bond. (Time marker 1:28:15, Chapter 15 on the DVD.) Hooper gains Quint's respect because Hooper instantly knows and understands what Quint went through on the *U.S.S. Indianapolis.* Hooper's breathless reaction to the mention of the name assures Quint of that. And because of his interests and studies, Hooper is probably one of the few who has an accurate concept of what the experience was like. He doesn't need the details to know Quint's horror story.

And Quint gains Hooper's respect because the oceanographer now knows that Quint learned everything about sharks from torturous, personal experience, not from some book or a safe, research study using all the latest safety and technical equipment. And like the rest of us, Hooper suddenly understands Quint's strange and crazy obsession.

That scene is the moment of <u>Change</u>, for both Hooper and Quint. Pay attention to the way they speak to each other the next day. Neither one had a personality transplant, but you get the feeling that, had Quint lived, they would have become enduring friends. Quint calls him "son" and tries to encourage and protect him. Quint's the one who asks what Hooper can do with his equipment. Very subtle, but the <u>Change</u> is there.

Note: During the entire "scars" conversation, Brody is on the outside, looking in. He checks out one of his own scars, considers hopping into the competition, then decides against it. He still doesn't belong.

From this point on, things happen quickly.

PACING

Light and sunny, people-filled chaotic scenes set one kind of pace in this movie. The threats develop gradually, and the audience sees them coming.

We hear the cellos begin their duh-duh duh-duh duh-duh Dun-dhuh and we know from witnessing the opening, that another shark attack is coming. But the attack surprises us anyway. After the first few times hearing that theme, we anticipate the shark and expect to be surprised *this* time by nothing happening. We think perhaps the dog will be eaten, but not the boy. Everyone will get out of the water. It's too bright and sunny for disaster. Disaster happens anyway.

During dark, shadowy, slower-paced, thoughtful scenes, we expect the worst. Instead, we learn things about the characters and/or the conflicts. We discover things and gain necessary information. Then something happens to startle us and make us jump: Hooper and Brody find the big hole in the fisherman's boat, and we jump as the head falls out of it. And we're surprised this time because nothing really happens. There's no disaster. No shark attack. No damage done that wasn't already done. No one gets attacked or eaten. We just get startled.

Story <u>Pace</u> is the speed at which things happen. Too slow a pace will kill an otherwise great story. Too fast a pace will prevent it from being memo-

QUICK TIP:

TRANSITIONS AS PACING

TRANSITIONS ARE ALWAYS USEFUL TO GET PAST THE BORING STUFF. LIKE EATING—AND OTHER BORING THINGS. USE TRANSITIONS TO GET FROM EVENT TO EVENT, SITUATION TO SITUATION. TRANSITIVE SENTENCES WILL GET YOU TO SEVERAL DAYS (OR EVEN TO FIVE MINUTES) FROM NOW. TRANSITIONING TO A NEW SCENE (HE GRABBED HIS KEYS AND HEADED FOR WORK. NEW PARAGRAPH. AT THE OFFICE . . .) WILL GET YOU FROM HOME ACROSS TOWN TO WORK—WITHOUT ALL THE BORING STUFF IN BETWEEN. (HE GRABBED HIS KEYS AND HEADED FOR HIS CAR. SETTLING INSIDE, HE FASTENED HIS SEATBELT, STARTED THE CAR AND BACKED OUT OF THE DRIVE. TRAFFIC WAS SLOW TODAY . . . .)

rable, because to maintain the breakneck pace, the writer sacrifices the details, background, and motivation that make a story great. Variety is the key to finding a "just right" pace that even Goldilocks would approve of.

Early in your book, your mix of scenes will lean toward a greater number of slower-paced ones. You are delivering a lot of information. That automatically slows you down. But you have to include fast-paced scenes, too, to keep the story unfolding at a satisfactory rate.

Naturally, when the reader knows your characters and the world you've created, the last half of the book will lean toward a heavier mix of fast-paced scenes. By now most of the must-have information has been given, and you're edging nearer toward an exciting resolution.

But a mix of fast- and slow-paced scenes is only part of the correct formula. Other elements also help you vary your pace. Dialogue quickens the pace. Introspection and reflection slows it down. Changing the mood—as we've seen in *Jaws*—from scene to scene also changes the pace. And pace feels breathless when you are being side-swiped by the unexpected, but not so surprising events because they are <u>Foreshadowed</u> and inevitable.

As Quint and Hooper finish their male-bonding with an appropriate drinking song, "Show Me the Way to Go Home," the shark attacks again. Inevitably he tries to eat the boat (*Peeling the Artichoke*: proving Brody totally right in his repeated assertions that they "need a bigger boat"). As they make repairs to the boat the next morning, the shark reappears. Brody goes to the radio to "make a phone call" for help. (We begin his <u>Reality</u> <u>Check</u>: He still wants to trust in something other than himself. He will definitely try all his options.) Quint smashes the radio to prevent the call.

Brody rages at him and calls him "certifiable." We don't doubt that Brody's right. But now we understand it. (This is Quint's <u>Reality</u> <u>Check</u>. Remember him saying he wouldn't put on a life preserver again? Not letting Brody call for help is a metaphor—a comparison—to that. Quint will not wait for help again. This time it will come down to either him or the shark. May the best man win!)

The shark attacks again; there is more damage to the boat. It's taking on water faster than Brody can pump it out and—with Quint's inadvertent help— the motor blows.

Quint throws Brody and Hooper life jackets and finally turns to Hooper. "What exactly can you do with these things of yours?" Quint asks. It's time for Hooper's <u>Reality</u> <u>Check</u>. Does he really believe all his knowledge, technical gadgets, and gimmicks can do what they've failed to do so far? He admits, as he goes into the water in his shark cage that he is so scared, he "ain't got no spit."

Seconds later the shark annihilates the cage, then turns his attention back to the boat. This attack takes off the back of the boat and Quint slowly slides right into his gaping jaws. With no help, no working radio, and a sinking ship, it's down to just Brody (<u>Black</u> <u>Moment</u>). The shark comes after him.

He tosses whatever is handy at the shark, including the compressed air tank. (Point #3 in the <u>Rule</u> <u>of</u> <u>Three</u>—we're not saying "yeah, sure" when the air tank is in the shark's mouth so that Brody can shoot it. Without the earlier picture and Hooper's warning about the air tank, we might have thought it was *lucky coincidence* that the air tank was what got stuck in his mouth when Brody was throwing everything but the kitchen sink at him.) With his gun, he climbs the mast as the ship sinks lower. There's no one, nothing left to depend on (<u>Ultimate</u> <u>Risk</u>). It's just him.

As the shark charges again, Brody says, "Smile, you son-of-a-bitch" Blam! And Brody proves he *is* capable (<u>Resolution</u>). He can go home now— where he's proved to himself he belongs—knowing he will be able to handle whatever responsibilities his job on an island entails.

Hooper surfaces; they paddle toward home as the credits begin to roll; and finally, we see two men in the distance, walking onto the shore to the tune of music much more mellow than the screeching strings we've been hearing since the shark first made its debut.

MAKING MUSIC WITH YOUR WORDS

Music is an asset movie makers have that writer's don't. When we hear cellos begin to play John William's classic duh-duh, we know the shark is on its way. The speed of the repetition picks up as the shark picks up the scent of its prey. The music has become so much a cliché, everyone recognizes it, wherever you hear it and no matter how badly someone sings it, as a warning.

At one of my workshops, a bestselling author asked what tool writers have at their disposal to use like a movie's score, as a warning, to set or enhance a mood, or to make a scene memorable. (Who can hear the song, "It's Raining Men," without remembering bodies flying in **Bridget Jones's Diary**?) At the time, I didn't have an answer. I do now.

Ironically, I discovered the answer listening to music—the words to the chorus of Rascal Flatts's song, "Everyday Love," to be specific.

I can't blame the light and happy feeling I get every time I hear the chorus strictly on the music, though I know that's part of it. Though I like this song, I'm not a great fan of country music. I love the lyrics. Obviously, the songwriters Danny Wells and Gene Nelson got out their thesaurus when they wrote it. And how much more plain, simple, and familiar can you get than using every synonym in the book for the word ordinary? But it worked to produce the satisfied, secure, and happy feeling I'm sure they wanted to convey.

The wonderful choices of the specific different words that have essentially the same meaning, and the repetition of them, produces the magic. And the words that struck me were from the chorus, so they get repeated several times.

I started watching for repetition when I read. In several books I found a specific phrase or sentence and, in several cases, even a single word used in a certain circumstance to set a mood or foreshadow what was coming. Check the way Dean Koontz used the word "whisper" in his book by the same name. Repetition is a wonderful technique. And bringing the same word or phrase back like a chorus makes it effective.

As is beat and meter. Comedians say timing is everything. And unless they are doing some type of slapstick or physical comedy, they, too, are restricted to words. Experiment with beat and meter to send a subtle message to the reader.

Experiment with longer or shorter words or phrases or sentences. Go ahead and get out the thesaurus, not so much for a specific word, but for a general one that would make a difference in tone or length and possibly change the beat of your writing. Read poetry. Reverse and rearrange a sentence until the beat feels right. This technique is partially pacing, but it's still the words that are important.

Play with word sounds. Some words sound harsh and kick-ass. Some sound soft and sly. Consciously choose words that clatter onto the scene (that start with k, p, q, t, d, a, or c) in paragraphs leading up to a big event. Try the opposite with soft and suspicious sounds (words that contain s, f, l. m, n, r, or c).

In Benchley's book, we don't have the duh-duh-duh-duh, but he used two techniques to give us a similar warning. He switched to the shark's point of view. In its point of view, we see the vast ocean around him first, and then the focus narrows, and narrows, and narrows again until its attention is strictly on the victim. Both of these techniques—point of view and narrowing focus—use words in the same way movies use music.

Writers have words. Only words. But words are very powerful things. We can tweak them, arrange and rearrange them, repeat them, use one alone or a string of them in a phrase or long sentence. And they can be as memorable as music.

I can't read "It is a truth universally acknowledged that a single man in possession of a good fortune must be in want of a wife . . ." without grinning with the same pleasure I felt reading Jane Austen's *Pride and Prejudice* for the very first time. I can't hear "It was the best of times, it was the worst of times," without feeling the incredible sob-my-eyes-out sadness I felt when I reached the end of Charles Dickens *A Tale of Two Cities*. I can't hear ". . . all men are created equal . . ." without feeling a swell of patriotic pride.

Words have power! Use them well and wisely.

Chapter Eleven

Parting Thoughts and Useful Stuff

I didn't want to leave you without passing on some of the things that I've found very helpful during the years, and a few last thoughts.

You'll find most of the books I referenced about writing in almost every good bookstore or library, though some are out of print. (Warning: Don't lend your writing favorites out to other writers. You'll never get them back. Writers are notorious for having a difficult time letting go of books.)

In the Appendices, you'll find the forms I've mentioned and a few others. If you visit my Web site, www.lightscamerafiction.com, you can print them out. There, you'll also find articles on a variety of topics such as Point of View and The Four Emotional Needs of Readers. I also have links to other sites I've found valuable. But the longer you write, the more you'll develop your own tools. These are just to give you ideas.

I briefly addressed this earlier, but how you use the lessons in this book will partially depend on the kind of writer you are.

In his book, *Writing Popular Fiction*, Dean Koontz suggests that writers sit down and type a sentence that will grab the reader's attention without a lot of thought or planning. He recommends that you do that again and again until you have one sentence or paragraph that intrigues and grabs you. "Shortly you will find yourself so interested in one of these hastily jotted openings that you won't rest until you've carried on with it."

I feel safe in assuming Koontz is a Seat-of-the-Pants (SOTP) writer. The SOTP writers I know write like this. They find an idea and then just sit down at their desk and go. They fly.

Many organizations and businesses call their Policy and Procedure manuals P&Ps. That's an appropriate designation for another type of writer. My P&P writer friends would happily write pages and pages of policies and procedures for their characters, but my P&P stands for Planner and Plotter.

P&P writers fill whole notebooks with scenes and sequels. Their characterization profiles are in-depth studies. They have pictures, cut from magazines, of their characters and blueprints of the house where their characters live. They draw layouts and maps of the town where their stories will take place. They are very formal about the whole process.

The P&P writer usually gets to to the end of his story with few surprises, and probably fewer glitches and has fewer revisions to do after he types "The End."

I'm Somewhere-in-Between (SIB) a SOTP and a P&P. We SIBs might get where we are going by planning a bit, then writing by the SOTP for the next part of the story. At some point, we may have to stop and do more planning before we go on.

I doubt you'll find a glaring difference in reading a book written by a SIB, a P&P, or a SOTP. I also doubt you'd be able to pick out which kind of writer is most prevalent.

No matter what kind of writer you are (unless you and your subconscious are extremely, extremely good), you will still have to revise to turn your story into a publishable one. Whether you're an SOTP, a P&P or an SIB, don't skimp on that aspect of writing. Your first draft is only the beginning.

Reluctance to revise is one of the common characteristics I've seen among those writers who didn't stick it out long enough to sell.

This book is about concepts. When I started writing, some things were easy. Some things were tough. Plotting is still hard work for me if you want to know the truth. When I quit thinking of it as story and began to think of it as a plan to fit all of the pieces together, it became a lot less intimidating.

The longer I wrote, the more I understood. I'd read a book or attend a conference or a writing workshop, and a particular author would explain something I'd been struggling with, and the light bulb would go off. I'd suddenly get it—at least better than I had. I never have figured out though, whether that particular person said "it" in a way that finally got through my preconceptions, or whether I was just ready to learn whatever it was.

I would bet you find that true for you, too. The more you write, the more you'll understand, even the things that are difficult for you now. And you'll learn them as you're ready—or when someone explains it the right way.

The whole point of this book is to offer visual examples you can study for yourself. I wanted to offer you a different take. Hopefully a few light bulbs have gone off. At the very least, maybe you've found a better understanding of some element of storytelling. If you still struggle with something, keep looking and keep writing. Sometime, someone—an author in a book on writing, or perhaps a workshop presenter at a writers' conference—will say "it" the way you need to hear it in order to finally "get" it.

The most important point I want to make is that the more you understand the different elements of a story and how they fit together, the better a writer you will be. When the planning and thinking is done, when it's time to write, that is exactly what you need to do. *Write* thinking about your story and your characters, not about whether you've put things in the right place, or whether your conflict is strong enough. That's *planning*. And evaluating how well you've executed the plan comes after you write. That's the *revision process*. It's not writing.

So now, put anything this book has helped you understand in the back of your brain. Forget about it and let your subconscious do its magic. *You go write!*

And let me know when your book is on the shelves at my local bookstore.

Recommended Resources

The Personality Self-Portrait: Why You Think, Work, Love, and Act the Way You Do by John M. Oldham, M.D., and Lois B. Morris

This book is invaluable for several reasons. It has a test that you can perform on your characters to find their personality type. The book goes into detail explaining each personality type's traits, both positive and negative. It's helpful in creating truly well-rounded characters.

American Chronicle: Six Decades in America, 1920–1980 by Lois Gordon and Alan Gordon's

If your stories are contemporary, this book is perfect for getting in touch with major characters and finding things that might have influenced them during their formative years. Figure out when they were born and then look, year by year, at what was happening in the world during that time: what was going on in the news and prices for a variety of common things—everything from pots and pans to gum and candy, and how much it cost to get a tooth filled. The book tells what was on the radio, TV, and the movies, and what music and books were popular. It has sports trivia, science and technology, fashion, fads, and odds and ends. You get a real feel for the kind of childhood your character probably had. There are other books that do the same, and I need my *own* update since some of my characters are too young for this book, but an almanac like this is priceless. Consider it the same kind of research historical or science-fiction writers do.

Any "name your baby" book is nice to have around, but my favorite is: *The Baby Name Personality Survey* by Bruce Lansky and Barry Sinrod.

Besides giving you the standard names and their meanings, the book provides information, based on surveys, about peoples' first impressions of a person, based solely on that person's name. That's very useful when you want your character to convey a certain image to the reader from the first introduction to him. It's almost imperative if you want to avoid giving a character a name that conveys the exact opposite image of the person you want that character to be.

A "body language" book is helpful but I haven't found the perfect one yet.

The Art of Readable Writing by Rudolf Flesch

This book will not help you develop characters or your story. It was originally published in 1949 and has been revised and reprinted numerous times.
(I'm not sure if it is still in print, but you can find copies on Amazon.com.) The
writing samples are extremely dated, but they make their points. It's geared
more to nonfiction writing than to fiction. The second half, especially, will
help you improve your writing because it gives you a better understanding
of what makes writing readable and turns it into an art. Many of the modern
computer programs that analyze what reading level a piece of writing is, are
based on this author's work. This book helps you understand how and why
those things are important.

CRITIQUE GROUPS

A critique group or partner is valuable in so many ways. Besides having
someone—other than your mother, who will always say it's good whether it
is or not—who will read your work and give you feedback, a critique partner
will understand exactly what you are going through because he is going
through the same thing. And you double your chances of catching problems
in your work or learning what you need to know about writing in general or
markets in particular. He'll know things you don't know and vice versa. Same
with his writing strengths and your weaknesses.

So where do writers find a critique group or partner? You have many
options. If you don't have time to meet face-to-face and exchange your comments and feedback, look online. Visit writers' sites. It won't take you long to
find another writer or two, willing to swap scenes or chapters for the benefit of your feedback on their work in progress. Join a local writers group. You
can find a variety on the Internet. Ask your local librarian. She or he will know

other writers in your area, and most likely has been approached by at least one in the past. If you don't find one close enough, post notes at your library, bookstore, or even at the grocery store, anywhere that has a public bulletin board. It may take a while to find the right partner or group, but you'll never find one if you don't actively look. Another great place to find other writers—ones who might want to critique with you—is at conferences or the types of writing classes offered in the non-credit schedule of almost any local university or junior college.

And remember that storytelling is storytelling. You don't have to find someone who is writing for the same markets as you are.

A FINAL TIP: TREAT YOURSELF LIKE A 'PROFESSIONAL'

IT'S THE ABSOLUTELY BEST THING YOU CAN DO—AND THE BEST TIP I CAN GIVE YOU—IF YOU TRULY WANT A CAREER IN WRITING. SET REGULAR HOURS, EVEN IF IT'S ONLY TWO HOURS A WEEK. DON'T MISS THEM. DO THE RESEARCH YOU NEED TO DO ON SUITABLE MARKETS FOR YOUR WORK. JOIN A WRITER'S GROUP. LEARN WHAT YOU NEED TO KNOW. SET UP YOUR OWN WRITER'S LIBRARY—EVEN IF IT'S ONE SHELF. THE MINUTE YOU TAKE YOUR DREAMS SERIOUSLY, THE PEOPLE AROUND YOU WILL DO THE SAME.

Conflict, motivation, characters—they are all essentials of any story regardless of genre.

Referenced Works

The Art of Dramatic Writing, Lajos Egris, Touchstone Books
(Simon and Schuster), 1946, New York, NY (revised 1960)

Blink: The Power of Thinking without Thinking
Malcolm Gladwell, Little, Brown and Co., 2005, New York, NY

Fiction Is Folks, Robert Newton Peck, Writer's Digest Books, 1983, Cincinnati, OH

How to Tell a Story: The Secrets of Writing Captivating Tales,
Gray Provost and Peter Rubie, Writer's Digest Books, 1998, Cincinnati, OH

Story: Substance, Structure, Style, and the Principles of Screenwriting,
by Robert McGee, Regan Books (Harper Publishers), 1997, New York, NY

Techniques of the Selling Writer, Dwigh Swain, 1965, assigned 1973,
University of Oklahoma Press, Norman, OK

Writing Popular Fiction, Dean Koontz, Writer's Digest Books, 1972, Cincinnati, OH

Writing Screenplays that Sell, Michael Hauge, Harper Perennial,
1991, New York, NY (originally published, McGraw-Hill, 1988, New York)

Appendix A

CHARACTER WORKSHEET

PHYSICAL

NAME _____

AGE _____ EYE COLOR _____ HAIR COLOR _____

HEIGHT _____ WEIGHT _____ BIRTH DATE _____

DISTINGUISHING MARKS _____

_____

_____

_____

_____

DIALOGUE TAG _____

PERSONAL GESTURE/TAG _____

PAST

RAISED BY _____

RAISED WHERE _____

WHAT WAS IMPORTANT TO THE PEOPLE WHO RAISED THIS CHARACTER?

_____

_____

_____

_____

_____

HOW DID THESE PEOPLE FEEL ABOUT THIS CHARACTER?

_____

_____

_____

_____

_____

SIBLINGS OR SIGNIFICANT OTHERS IN THE HOUSEHOLD

_____

_____

_____

_____

_____

ECONOMIC/SOCIAL STATUS

_____

_____

_____

_____

_____

_____

RELIGIOUS/MORAL   _____

BACKGROUND   _____

_____

_____

_____

_____

EDUCATIONAL BACKGROUND   _____

_____

_____

_____

_____

_____

WHAT INCIDENTS/SITUATIONS   _____

SHAPED THE CHARACTER'S   _____

MAIN TRAITS   _____

_____

_____

WHAT INCIDENTS/SITUATIONS   _____

MOST INFLUENCED THIS   _____

CHARACTER FOR GOOD?   _____

_____

_____

_____

WHAT INCIDENTS/SITUATIONS
MOST INFLUENCED THIS
CHARACTER FOR ILL?

_____
_____
_____
_____
_____

PRESENT

WHAT THREE CHARACTER
TRAITS RULE THE CHARACTER'S
ACTIONS (OR INACTIONS)?

_____
_____
_____
_____
_____

WHAT DOES THIS CHARACTER
WANT MOST RIGHT NOW?

_____
_____
_____
_____
_____

RESIDENCE? HOW DOES THIS
CHARACTER SEE HERSELF AND
HER SURROUNDINGS?

_____
_____
_____
_____
_____
_____

WHOM DOES THE CHARACTER
LIVE WITH/WORK WITH/SEE
REGULARLY?

_____

_____

_____

_____

_____

EVEN IF THESE PEOPLE WILL
NOT BE A PART OF THE STORY,
HOW DO THEY SEE THE
CHARACTER?

_____

_____

_____

_____

_____

IF THESE PEOPLE ARE
IMPORTANT TO THIS STORY,
HOW? WHY?

_____

_____

_____

_____

_____

OCCUPATION

_____

HOW DOES THIS CHARACTER
SEE HIMSELF IN REGARDS TO
HIS OCCUPATION?

_____

_____

_____

_____

HOW DO THE OTHER PEOPLE
WHO ARE PART OF THE STORY
SEE THIS CHARACTER? WHY?

_____
_____
_____
_____
_____

INTERESTS/PASSIONS

_____
_____
_____
_____
_____

WHAT ARE THIS CHARACTER'S
THREE MOST OBVIOUS
STRENGTHS?

_____
_____
_____
_____
_____

WHAT ARE HIS MOST OBVIOUS
WEAKNESSES?

_____
_____
_____
_____
_____

FUTURE

**WHAT IS THIS CHARACTER'S
DREAM FOR THE FUTURE?**

_____
_____
_____
_____
_____

**DOES HE BELIEVE THAT HIS
DREAMS ARE ACHIEVABLE?
(WHY OR WHY NOT?)**

_____
_____
_____
_____
_____

**WHAT DOES THIS CHARACTER
MOST WANT IN THE FUTURE?**

_____
_____
_____
_____
_____

**HOW FAR IS THIS CHARACTER
WILLING TO GO TO GET IT?**

_____
_____
_____
_____
_____

Appendix B

CHARACTER GOALS AND OBSTACLES WORKSHEET

WHAT DOES THE CHARACTER
WANT? (THE GOAL)
_____
_____
_____

WHY DOES HE WANT IT?
(THE MOTIVATION)
_____
_____
_____

HOW BADLY DOES HE WANT IT?
HOW FAR WILL HE
GO TO GET IT?
_____
_____
_____

WHAT INITIAL OBSTACLE
DOES HE FACE?
_____
_____
_____

DOES THE CHARACTER HAVE A
PLAN FOR GETTING WHATEVER
IT IS? IF SO,
WHAT'S THE PLAN?

_____
_____
_____
_____
_____
_____

WHY DOES THIS CHARACTER
WANT THIS THING?

_____
_____
_____
_____
_____
_____
_____

WHAT SHORT AND MID-TERM GOALS MUST HE REACH TO OVERCOME THE INITIAL OBSTACLE?

_____

_____

_____

_____

WHAT DOES HE LEARN FROM HIS SUCCESS OR FAILURE?

_____

_____

_____

WHAT IS THE NEXT OBSTACLE HE FACES? (REPEAT FOR EACH NEW OBSTACLE.)

_____

_____

_____

WHAT ARE THE SHORT-AND/OR MID-TERM GOALS HE MUST REACH? (REPEAT FOR EACH)

_____

_____

_____

DOES HE MEET SUCCESS OR FAILURE? (REPEAT FOR EACH)

_____

_____

_____

WHAT FINAL OBSTACLE MUST BE OVERCOME?

_____

_____

_____

DOES THE PROTAGONIST
REACH HIS GOAL? WHY OR
WHY NOT?

_____

_____

_____

_____

Appendix C

PEELING THE ARTICHOKE WORKSHEET

OLD BELIEF: THE INFERIORITY COMPLEX

_____

_____

_____

WHAT BELIEF DOES THIS CHARACTER HAVE TO CHANGE ABOUT HIMSELF TO REACH HIS INTERNAL GOAL?

_____

_____

_____

WHAT REVEALS THE BELIEF TO THE READER?

_____

_____

_____

HOW IS THE BELIEF REINFORCED IN THE CHARACTER'S (AND THE READER'S) MIND? NAME SPECIFIC EVENTS OR SITUATIONS.

_____

_____

_____

WHAT HAPPENS (IDEALLY THREE THINGS) THAT WILL MAKE THE READER BEGIN TO QUESTION THE OLD BELIEF AND WONDER IF IT'S TRUE? (IT MAY BE A TOTAL SUCCESS, BUT THE HERO CAN'T TAKE FULL CREDIT, OR IT CAN BE A PARTIAL SUCCESS AND THE HERO CAN TAKE ALL OF THE CREDIT FOR THE PIECE THAT WAS SUCCESSFUL.)

_____

_____

_____

WHAT HAPPENS (AT LEAST ONE EVENT, BUT PREFERABLY SEVERAL) THAT WILL FULLY UNDERMINE THE HERO'S ORIGINAL BELIEF AND FORM THE BASIS FOR HIS NEW BELIEF? (THESE CAN BE CREDITED _ONLY_ TO THE HERO.)

_____

_____

_____

WHAT IS THE FINAL TEST TO THE NEW BELIEF THE CHARACTER NOW HOLDS? (ONCE HE PASSES THE FINAL TEST, HE CAN NO LONGER HOLD THE PREVIOUS BELIEF.)

_____

_____

_____

NEW BELIEF: INTERNAL GOAL ACHIEVED

_____

_____

_____

_____

_____

Appendix D

TEN-STEP PLOT PLANNER FOR A FIVE-STAR PLOT

STEP #1. ESTABLISH CHARACTERS AND GOALS

_____

_____

_____

_____

STEP #2. BEGIN WITH SCENES THAT INTRODUCE CHARACTERS, SETTING, TONE, AND THE PROBLEM THAT LEADS TO CHANGE.

_____

_____

_____

_____

STEP #3. 1ST PIVOTAL POINT: CHARACTER DECISION

_____

_____

_____

STEP #4. SCENES FURTHER DEVELOP THE CHARACTER AND SHOW HIM FACING OBSTACLES THAT BRING SOME SETBACKS BUT MOSTLY SUCCESS. ESTABLISH SECONDARY CHARACTERS AND STORYLINES.

_____

_____

_____

_____

STEP #5. 2ND PIVOTAL POINT: FAILURE

_____

_____

_____

_____

STEP #6. SCENES SHOW THE CHARACTER RENEWING HIS DETERMINATION AND MAKING CHANGES THAT WILL LEAD TO SUCCESS. THE OBSTACLES ARE LARGER AND THE SUCCESSES HARDER TO COME BY, BUT THE CHARACTER GROWS.

_____

_____

_____

_____

STEP #7. 3RD PIVOTAL POINT: REAL RISK.

_____

_____

_____

_____

STEP #8. SCENES CONCLUDE SECONDARY STORYLINES AND TIE UP LOOSE ENDS. THE CHARACTER SHOWS REAL CHANGE, BUT THE GROWTH IS TESTED, LEADING TO THE BLACK MOMENT.

_____

_____

_____

_____

STEP #9. CHARACTER TAKES THE ULTIMATE RISK.

_____

_____

_____

_____

STEP #10. RESOLUTION: THE CHARACTER REACHES (OR DOESN'T REACH) HIS GOAL AND ACHIEVES SUCCESS.

_____

_____

_____

_____

Appendix E

FIVE-STAR PLOT CHECKLIST

THE BEGINNING

MAIN CHARACTER   _____

PROBLEM   _____

SETTING   _____

TONE   _____

DECISION   _____

1ST PIVOTAL POINT

CHARACTERIZATION   _____

SECONDS   _____

SETBACKS   _____

SUCCESSES   _____

FAILURE   _____

2ND PIVOTAL POINT

RENEWAL _____

SUCCESSES _____

OBSTACLES _____

GROWTH _____

REAL RISK _____

3RD PIVOTAL POINT

SECONDS _____

CHARACTER CHANGE _____

REALITY CHECK _____

BLACK MOMENT _____

ULTIMATE RISK _____

Appendix F

ONE-PAGE STORY SYNOPSIS

BEGIN WITH A ONE-SENTENCE PERSONALIZED STORY PREMISE QUESTION.

(CAN CHER STOP WANDERING AROUND CLUELESS, QUIT GIVING HERSELF SNAPS FOR MEDDLING

IN—AND MESSING UP—OTHER PEOPLES LIVES, AND FIND DIRECTION FOR HER OWN?)

_____

_____

NEXT PARAGRAPH: INTRODUCE STRONGEST MOTIVATING CHARACTER TRAIT/INTERNAL GOAL, STORY SETTING, AND THE PROBLEM,

WRITTEN IN THE TONE OF YOUR STORY. END WITH THE CHARACTER'S DECISION AND EXTERNAL GOAL.

_____

_____

_____

_____

NEXT PARAGRAPH: SHOW THE FIRST MAJOR OBSTACLE AND THE CRUSHING FAILURE AT THE 1ST PIVOTAL POINT.

_____

_____

_____

_____

_____

NEXT PARAGRAPH: SHOW THE CHARACTER'S RENEWED DETERMINATION TO REACH THE GOAL, SOME CHARACTER GROWTH, AND HIS REAL RISK.

_____

_____

_____

_____

_____

NEXT PARAGRAPH: SHOW THE CHARACTER'S CHANGE, THE ULTIMATE RISK, AND BLACK MOMENT.

_____

_____

_____

_____

_____

ONE SENTENCE SUMMARY OF THE RESOLUTION.

_____

_____

Acknowledgments

All sorts of people helped me write this book. Needless to say, I cannot name—or even remember—some I probably should praise, credit or at least thank. And where would I start? With my mother and father for giving me life and any skills or talents I possess? My brothers, sisters, uncles, aunts, cousins, friends, past and present, for their part in teaching me the fine art of analysis, argument, writing or life? Even random strangers gave me encouragement, support, or comments that set some invaluable train of thought chugging along in my writer's brain. Don't worry. I won't name them all but there are a few I must. Without their help, this book wouldn't be.

I owe a debt of gratitude and more to Michael Hauge, for helping to plant the seed with his wonderful seminars. (I went twice.)

Gwen Duzenberry, a wonderful writer, an even truer friend and a gentle but always insightful critic: Thank you for helping me nurture the seed and take it from tiny sprout to full-grown finished product. I'll never know how to thank you or what I would do without you.

Kathy Carmichael, the left side of my brain when that side isn't working and the right side of it when only the left side is working. Who could ask for a more incredible friend or a more intuitive critic? And a talented author besides! Your Quick Tips and Quick Fixes—whether for my life or my writing—are always what I need, exactly when I need them.

To my other critics, John Banka, Cheryl Mansfield, Joyce Soule, Candy Cole, Sharon Flannery, and DeAnn Sicard: thanks for your valuable and astute feedback.

To Mark Carson, whose technical knowledge was superb but whose random act of kindness was especially needed when I was in crisis mode. Thanks especially for the reminder all over again that people, in general, are good and kind. I will Pay It Forward as often as I can.

To Stephanie Rosten and Jennifer Kasius: thank you for your belief in this project and your help in getting it off the ground. Lisa Clancy, you are a joy to work with. Thanks for helping me make this the best book it could be. Seta Bedrossian, Matt Goodman, John R. Douglas, and Joelle Herr lent assistance with the same goal in mind. To all at Levine, Greenberg and Running Press who went out of their way to help: I hope I remembered to thank you at the time. Sometimes my head is full of whatever we've been working on and I wonder later if I offered my gratitude. I offer it now. Please know your efforts were and are appreciated.

And last but never least, Drew, my son, my very favorite movie critic, and verbal sparring partner—you keep me thinking; and Danedri, my daughter, my very favorite optimist and columnist—you inspire me. You keep me sane.

Dan, the almost perfect mold for a writer's soulmate: "Get in there and write," he says when I need a nudge. "Go write," he says when I look reluctantly at the growing pile of laundry or the floor that hasn't been swept in two weeks. "I'll do that." He knows how to be silent when I need silence. He knows how to listen when I need to talk—though, being a man and not a writer, he doesn't always know what to say back. But the important part is listening. He knows everything there is to know about support, encouragement and love. And he's darn good at seeing "the inevitable" in movies. Thanks forever, Dan.

To God, for all Your promises—which You always keep.

Jeremiah 29:10-11

About
the Author

After holding a variety of jobs and operating several small businesses, Alfie Thompson finally realized what she wanted to be when she grew up, and she started writing. She's been addicted ever since. Her first book was written on a typewriter in a "cubby hole" (a converted stairwell off her kitchen) after her children were asleep at night. Ten novels (written as Val Daniels) later, she loves sharing what she has learned almost as much as she enjoys writing, and has presented workshops from New York City to Hawaii. With two-and-a-half million of her books in print worldwide, it delights the part of her that made her a writer to know she can communicate in many languages she can neither speak nor read.

Alfie grew up in south-central Kansas, married the Prince Charming she met in college, and had two children, who are grown and considering writing projects of their own. She resides near Kansas City with her husband, Dan.

Please visit her Web site: www.lightscamerafiction.com